THE RECTOR AND THE ROGUE

BOOKS BY W. A. SWANBERG

Sickles the Incredible (1956)
First Blood: The Story of Fort Sumter (1957)
Jim Fisk: The Career of an Improbable Rascal (1959)
Citizen Hearst: A Biography of William Randolph Hearst (1961)
Dreiser (1965)
Pulitzer (1967)
The Rector and The Rogue (1968)
Luce and His Empire (1972)
Norman Thomas: The Last Idealist (1976)
Whitney Father, Whitney Heiress (1980)

THE RECTOR

and

THE ROGUE

BY

W. A. SWANBERG

EDITED AND WITH AN AFTERWORD BY

PAUL COLLINS

THE COLLINS LIBRARY
[A DIV. OF McSWEENEY'S BOOKS]

McSWEENEY'S BOOKS
SAN FRANCISCO

www.mcsweeneys.net

The Collins Library is a series of newly edited and typeset editions
of unusual out-of-print books. It is an imprint of McSweeney's,
a privately held company with wildly fluctuating resources.

Editor: Paul Collins
Assistant Editor: Jennifer Elder

ISBN: 978-1-936365-23-4

CONTENTS

I.   INTIMATIONS OF ROGUERY 9

II.   THE CENTER OF GRAVITY 17

III. ENTER GENTLEMAN JOE 29

IV. MALICIOUS MONKEY TRICKS 37

V.   OLD IRELAND FOREVER! 43

VI. FOLLOW THAT CHOIRMASTER! 55

VII. SUBTLETIES OF JOKESMANSHIP 63

VIII. THE CIRCUS WILL BEGIN AT 8½ 75

IX. TRINITY'S GIN MILLS AND BROTHELS 81

X.   HOT ON THE TRAIL 93

XI. THE VILLAIN AT BAY 103

XII. GENIUS BEHIND BARS 113

XIII. THE CONFEDERATE AGENT 125

XIV. EXPANDING TALENTS 135

XV. THE THORNY PATH I TREAD 145

XVI. THE DUKE OF SING SING 155

AUTHOR'S NOTE 167

AFTERWORD 177

This scandalous tale is dedicated to Betty & Carter

CHAPTER I

INTIMATIONS OF ROGUERY

If the Reverend Dr. Morgan Dix, rector of Trinity Parish in New York City, had been so benighted as to believe in pixies, he would have sworn they were abroad on that otherwise pleasant Wednesday, February 18, 1880. The most mysterious and appalling visitation that ever befell him was foreshadowed by a cloud no bigger than a small child's hand. In his mail that morning he received one letter that puzzled him. It was from the Acme Safe Company in downtown Manhattan, whose manager thanked him for his inquiry, enclosed a price list along with literature describing a complete line of office safes and said that a representative would call.

Although his parish property was valued in the millions, the rector left the husbanding of it to others. He needed no safe and had addressed no such inquiry. He had his secretary write the Acme manager explaining that an error had been made and asking him not to bother sending a salesman on a useless errand. The letter was hardly mailed before the Acme man, sporting splendid mutton-chop whiskers, bounded up the brownstone stairs and rang the bell. He seemed astonished when Dr. Dix told him of the error, saying that he had seen the letter of inquiry and was certain of the name and address, but he apologized for what apparently was a misunderstanding and left.

Not ten minutes later the bell rang again. This time the caller was a bespectacled, middle-aged man who identified himself as a faculty member of St. John's School for Girls on West Thirty-second Street. He spoke glowingly of St. John's School, handed the rector a brochure, said that he could not possibly do better than to place his charges there and suggested that they discuss it in detail in the sitting room. The rector told him that since his only child, Catherine Morgan Dix, was not quite two years old, he was not yet ready to select a school for her. His visitor eyed him queerly, produced a postcard from his pocket and handed it over. Addressed to St. John's School and penned in a hasty hand, it read:

> Dear Sirs: Having received good reports of your institution, and having twenty wards of the parish I wish to place in school, I would appreciate full information as to your rates and arrangements. Wonderful day, is it not? Resp'y,
>
> Rev. Morgan Dix.

Dr. Dix's mouth tightened into the straight line it always formed when he was confronted by dishonesty. The letter was a forgery, he said, explaining that someone, apparently a practical joker, must be mailing such requests in his name. He added, one may safely surmise, that he was not in the habit of including such breezy gossip about the weather in his business correspondence. The caller, surprised and disappointed, gave him the postcard as evidence. As he left, a burly individual wearing rough clothing and a dented derby hat rounded the corner from Broadway, led two handsome bays up recently asphalted Twenty-fifth Street and tied them with a flourish at the Dix hitching post. He spat a stream of tobacco juice into the gutter before he addressed the rector as "Your Reverend" and said he was from Van Tassel & Kearney, horse auctioneers on East Thirteenth Street. He urged the Reverend to look closely at these two beautiful examples of horseflesh. The bays, he said, were the best matched pair of carriage horses in the city, five years old, perfectly trained, gentle as lambs, not frightened in the least by the Elevated—in short, just what the Reverend had asked for.

Dr. Dix's lips formed that straight line again. He had asked for no horses, he said. He was entirely satisfied with the pair he had. Sure enough, Van Tassel & Kearney had received another forged postcard on which some imp of Satan impersonating the rector wrote of needing a pair promptly, for use on Washington's Birthday, and finished with impetuous good cheer, "May happiness be with you!"

In his afternoon mail were a dozen letters from local dealers in safes, locks, stoves and kitchenware, all of them under the impression that he had written them commenting favorably on their merchandise and saying he was planning to buy in large quantities for church, orphanage and mission use. G. Rauschfuss, a Twelfth Street maker of wigs and toupees, arrived expecting to fit him for a headpiece, and a man from Cartier's Dancing Academy on Union Square, having been informed by postcard that Trinity Parish wished to instruct twenty-five Sunday School teachers in the waltz, was delighted to offer special low group rates and an assurance that six lessons would suffice except for outright clodhoppers. This last particularly irked Dr. Dix, who thought dancing to be sinful. In fact, this peculiar campaign of botheration promised not only to waste his time but to threaten his reputation, since the postcards passed through many hands and there was no telling how many people might read and believe such things about him as that he wore a toupee and encouraged church-school teachers to dance.

It reminded him of a like incident of the previous autumn. In mid-September of 1879, an Episcopal colleague whom he knew well but not intimately, the Reverend Dr. Randolph McKim, rector of Holy Trinity Church in Harlem, had received the following note:

Reverend and Dear Sir: Your card in the New-York *Herald* is certainly a mistake. You call for a centennial celebration of the adoption of the Common Prayer-book; but the Common Prayer-book was not adopted in 1779 but in 1785. Pardon me for correcting this mistake, and believe me, very truly yours,

Morgan Dix.

Dr. McKim, not familiar with Dix's handwriting, was taken aback because he had published no card in the *Herald* or any other newspaper. He wrote Dr. Dix saying that he could not understand his letter. Dix's reply in turn expressed surprise, saying he was at a loss to comprehend McKim's letter. McKim, who had torn up the previous note about the "centennial celebration," fished the pieces out of his wastebasket, pasted them together and sent the epistolary mosaic to Dr. Dix by way of explanation. Dix wrote back, assuring him that the letter was a forgery and that someone was making game with them both. There the matter rested until October twenty-eighth, when Dr. Dix received a postcard addressed impertinently, "Rev. Morgan Dix, candidate for Assistant Bishop of New York," and reading:

D'r Sir, D'r Sir: In reply, would say, I regret to say I cannot support you, my choice being Rev. Mr. Morrill of St. Alban's Church, my second choice being Rev. Father Hall of Boston. Regret not being able to oblige you. Yours truly,

R. McKim, Harlem, N.Y., Oct. 27, 1879.

The message's handwriting made it evident to Dr. Dix that the same witling was at work. He sent the card back to McKim and the two agreed to be on their guard against such drollery. However, nothing further occurred and Dr. Dix had forgotten the incident until now, four months later, when a more ambitious campaign of confusion was directed against him by the same conspirator, as indicated by the handwriting.

The letters and personal calls he received from deluded tradespeople on February eighteenth were as nothing compared with those the following day. February twentieth, a Friday, showed another increase, with an armload of mail that made the postman stagger and a parade of callers now representing an expanded list of commercial enterprises. Among them were four dealers in church organs, one of whom had come all the way from Boston, and three salesmen of farming equipment (one just off the train from Philadelphia) who were under the impression that the rector was interested in buying reapers and threshing machines for a mythical upstate farm operated by the church for the benefit of the poor. In the mail were free samples of breakfast food, tinned beef, soap, shoe polish, compressed yeast, condensed milk, corn remedies and many different kinds of patent medicines. The letters, which on the first day had come only from New York, now poured in from points as distant as Buffalo, Detroit, Milwaukee, Chicago, Cincinnati and St. Louis. They were written by dealers in a wide assortment of merchandise ranging from underwear to fire extinguishers, punch presses, metal lathes and 300-horsepower steam engines. Dr. Dix, who was not entirely without humor and had met the first day's siege with a shade of amusement mixed with sympathy for his perplexed callers, was beginning to look a trifle worn.

"It is surprising," he said, "that the very conveniences of civilization can be made the source of so much vexation and annoyance."

This time-consuming moonshine put him in arrears in his parish work. He was having trouble completing his sermon for Sunday.

Although he could have stationed a servant at the door to turn away callers, he did it himself because he felt it his duty to make explanations to them personally and he wanted to question them for possible clues to the identity of his tormentor. He made no headway in this, since no one had seen the forger; all had been misled by postcards falsely signed with Dix's name. He collected many of the postcards, finding them written in the same hasty hand. He had first sent personal replies to those firms addressing him by mail, but when the letters multiplied he took refuge in a printed form reply explaining the situation and asking that any communications signed in his name be sent to him.

He hoped that the jokester would tire of the game—a wish that Saturday did not fulfill, for the stream of letters and visitors increased that day to a flood, coming now from new industrial areas including makers of pianofortes and band instruments, plumbing equipment and mausoleums, and publishers of Bibles and hymnals.

Sunday was a holy day twice over because it meant a cessation of spoken and written importunities that he buy something. It was Washington's one hundred and forty-eighth birthday, traditionally reserved for honoring the military with services in which Morgan Dix, who had buried his soldier father only the previous year, always entered with sincere feeling. That morning, eighty-four-year-old General Abram Daily led seven tottering old men, the last remnant of the local Veterans of the War of 1812, into St. Paul's Church at Broadway and Fulton Street—one of Trinity's chapels—and sat them down in the sacred pew once occupied by George and Martha Washington. They were expecting that Dr. Dix would preach the sermon for them—a duty he would have cherished because his late father had long been leader of the dwindling group. But liaison had broken down somewhere because of the grueling four days the rector had spent. One of his assistants, the Reverend Dr. James Mulcahey, pastor at St. Paul's, welcomed the veterans and announced in embarrassment that there had been "some oversight" and he had not known until then that they would attend St. Paul's that day. It was the sort of contretemps that Dr. Dix, a stickler for efficiency, would never have permitted under ordinary circumstances, but the veterans had to make do with Dr. Mulcahey's hastily revised sermon.

That afternoon, a group of sixty comparatively boyish veterans of the Civil War laid a wreath on the statue of Washington in Union Square, then marched smartly to Trinity Church, where Dr. Dix preached for them and a large congregation as the great bells in the tower ceased their tintinnabulation. He took for his text a passage from Matthew, XI that was almost as apt a commentary on his own troubles as on the need for vigilant defense: "And from the days of John the Baptist until now the kingdom of heaven suffereth violence and the violent take it by force."

CHAPTER II

THE CENTER OF GRAVITY

During his eighteen years as rector of Trinity Parish, Morgan Dix had weathered a succession of crises ranging from the violent, when a demented man had blazed away with a pistol during communion services, to the libelous, when a freethinkers' newspaper had peremptorily accused Trinity of harboring seven hundred and sixty-four gin mills and ninety-six brothels in its New York property. By 1880 he might have been forgiven for a comfortable feeling that it would take something extraordinary to shake his aplomb.

There had been surprise and even disapproval when the vestry elected him rector in 1862 over the heads of older ministers of the parish, some of whom were themselves wounded by the slap at seniority. The most grievously wounded was the Reverend Dr. Francis Vinton, who was eighteen years older, a graduate of West Point and a practicing lawyer before he studied for the priesthood—a clergyman of such prestige that he had twice been a leading candidate for a bishopric. Dix, who for a time had been Vinton's assistant, knew he felt like the prime minister displaced by a footboy, but handled the situation with such diplomacy that Vinton stayed on in reasonable contentment until he died.

Externally Dix was solemn, reserved, as cold as a mackerel. When the small daughter of a clergyman friend of his was asked by her father about her lessons: "Have you found out what is the center of gravity?" she replied, "Yes! Dr. Dix." If it was an exaggeration to say that the chill emanating from his person could cause frostbite, it *could* at any rate cause gooseflesh. This seemed to be an unintended outward and priestly mannerism. When he was off duty and among friends, his demeanor could melt into warmest geniality.

Born an aristocrat, he had proved himself the perfect choice for a congregation largely composed of aristocrats. The aristocratic George Templeton Strong, who had been a Trinity vestryman until his death in 1875, was a finicky fellow with a passion for character dissection who stayed not his gift for sarcasm in commenting on the stupidity or sleep-inducing sermons of other priests of the parish. About Dix he was downright enthusiastic, describing him as "a brick of the first quality," and saying, "I never knew a more genuine man, or one who can be cultivated with more pleasure and profit." In addition, he was right on top of probably the most exacting clerical job anywhere. Trinity Parish was the oldest, wealthiest and most fashionable in the country, a startling amalgam of capitalism and Christianity, owner of so much property in the heart of Manhattan that it had its own corporation to control it. The property, worth about $8,000,000 in 1880, appreciated every year so that Dr. Dix would live to see it reach $75,000,000. The immense income it returned annually was used for philanthropy and charity as well as for the propagation of the gospel at Trinity Church, whose 284-foot gothic tower at Broadway and Wall Street—the highest structure in the city—dominated the stock market and the money men. Under Trinity were six subsidiary parish chapels scattered through the city, each of them sizable. The rector was governor of a complicated domain, both ecclesiastical and secular, that required him to be a good business man as well as outstanding in churchmanship. Morgan Dix was so accomplished at both that his frozen face could be forgiven. In addition to expending endless effort in improving his parishioners' immortal souls, he could add a column of figures, understand a legal brief, give heed to the pennies in the children's collection as well as the millions in the church coffers, keep a firm hand over fourteen assistant ministers, treat tactfully with a board of vestrymen who did not always see eye to eye and in general work like a drayhorse without showing signs of wear.

That is, he showed no signs of wear until 1880, the year of the letters, when he came near wearing out in a month's time.

Fifty-two years old, spare, so erect and proud in bearing that he made his less-than-middle height seem almost impressive, he parted his rather lank gray hair on the side and peered through pince-nez with severity tempered by kindly lines around the eyes. "You can see by his face," one observer noted, "that he is determined to keep the devil down." He loathed sensationalism in the pulpit, which is to say that he was contemptuous of his two noisy Brooklyn contemporaries, Henry Ward Beecher of Plymouth Church and Dr. T. De Witt Talmage of the Brooklyn Tabernacle. His sermons bore on matters spiritual, not temporal—on the soul rather than on politics. To Dix, Beecher's belief in evolution and in women's suffrage were heretical and dangerous. To Dix, who came from generations of Episcopalians and would remain an Episcopalian even if he were the only one left, Talmage's switch from the Dutch Reformed to the Presbyterian Church must have seemed raw expediency, and the love of publicity that drove Talmage, while visiting in Palestine, to baptize a man in the Jordan, a profanation. While Talmage published such books as *The Night Sides of City Life*, and *Social Dynamite*, or, *The Wickedness of Modern Society*, Dix's publications ran to such topics as *A Commentary on the Epistle to the Romans*, and *Lectures on the Pantheistic Idea of an Impersonal-Substance Deity*. While Dix preached the gospel, Talmage orated about the horrors of dissipation and got Monday-morning newspaper headlines never given the metaphysical man of Trinity.

Nor would Dix *ever* get the kind of headlines Beecher won daily during his long, indecisive trial for adultery with Elizabeth Tilton. That trial was almost five years gone and yet in a sense never ended, continuing for every remaining year of Beecher's life and still sending shock waves into the whole churchly establishment. Let Beecher and Talmage posture like politicians or vaudeville performers; Dr. Dix would continue to stress the Church Year and to elevate the Holy Eucharist for his own parish. He could have preached a dozen sermons on the sensationalist Beecher who finally became the top sensation of all, the trapper who stumbled into the jaws of his own trap, but of course he did not. Too sensational. As will be seen, his almost morbid abhorrence of publicity made him a particularly vulnerable victim of whoever was sending those letters.

While he was as smug and stern morally as Cotton Mather, he was not without some flexibility. For example, many clergymen frowned on croquet, which had swept the country since its introduction from England, on several grounds. It encouraged the mingling of the sexes in a sporting contest—something that had never happened before; it was felt undignified for women to acknowledge that they were bipeds, or to exhibit in public the exertion demanded by croquet, or to bend over, or to separate the feet (even though the feet were all but hidden by hoopskirts) as was necessary if one were to take a good swipe at the ball. Dix, on the other hand, wielded a joyful mallet in mixed company although of course he took for granted perfect feminine dignity. Croquet was as much a social function as a game, and socially he was charming the moment he got away from God and was given companions not too far removed in status, background and intelligence. His graces of hospitality had been polished by a sociable family circle and frequent travel even before his ministry put a final gloss on them. He had been everywhere in Europe, always with profit. He knew the classics and was knowledgeable in music and art. (His youngest brother, Charles Temple Dix, who had died of consumption in Rome in 1873, had been an accomplished painter.) The wiles of politics were known to him and occasionally useful in parish work. If his sense of humor was underdeveloped, he sought to compensate by telling jokes he knew to be amusing because of their very atrociousness, such as one he sprang on several pillars of his own church: "What is the difference between a vestryman and a street loafer?" Answer: "The former passes the saucer, while the latter sauces the passer."

It had to be said that the rector was unconscionably fossilized in doctrine and a bit of an involuntary snob. He supervised extensive benefits for the underprivileged, never knowing that he could not refer to "the poor" or "the working classes" except with patronization. Money meant little to him simply because he took it for granted, as he took for granted a staff of servants and other luxuries. His family had always been wealthy and he would inherit a tidy fortune. His $4,000 starting salary at Trinity had been steadily raised to $10,000, plus the use of a handsome rectory. He had reached the highest attainable power and position of the priestly office, a power beyond most bishops. He was so content with this that he consistently declined flattering offers, such as a professorship at Columbia College, consideration for a bishopric and the presidency of a seminary for clergymen.

Happy, happy man! A biblical student might reflect that such inordinate well-being, like that of Job, with his thousands of sheep, camels, oxen and asses, made the practice of Christianity easy, and that the astonishing crisis he was soon to face was as necessary for his soul as the tribulations of Job.

He was proud of his father, the sawed-off but phenomenal John

Adams Dix, who had performed the improbable feat of holding an officer's commission both in the War of 1812 (ensign) and the Civil War (major general). The general had lived his long life at constant top speed. He had served variously as state assemblyman, New York Secretary of State, United States Senator, postmaster in New York City, Secretary of the Treasury (during his tenure of which office he lived in the White House for the last six weeks of Buchanan's administration), departmental commander during the war, Minister to France, governor of New York and president of three railroads, the Rock Island, Erie and Union Pacific. Along the way, he carried on a law practice, dabbled in art and architecture, played the piano with skill, wrote facile poetry, executed solid translations of Martial and Claudian, said his prayers in Latin, tried earnestly to become President of the United States and enjoyed shooting ducks on Long Island. Thus Morgan Dix had enjoyed all the advantages of wealth, social position and a dazzling cultural background. Through his home from boyhood on had trooped congressmen, senators, Cabinet members and ranking military officers, not to mention prelates, professors, musicians and artists. His parents had known Presidents Polk, Pierce and Johnson, had been quite close to Buchanan, and for two and a half years had been welcome at the palace of Napoleon III and Empress Eugénie, who presented them with two splendid Sevres vases.

Born in 1827 in New York City, Morgan Dix had spent part of his boyhood in Cooperstown and Albany and in European travel, studying art and the classics in Italy. He returned to his birthplace when he was eighteen to enter Columbia College, then a small appendage of Trinity Parish housed in one building off Church Street. Graduating with honors in 1848, he declined an appointment to West Point not because he was opposed to soldiership, which he regarded as an honorable profession in an imperfect world, but because at twenty-one he considered himself too old, recalling that his father had won an ensign's commission at the age of fourteen. He read law at the general's suggestion that it was the best training for the career of politics and public service contemplated for him, and he studied politics at first hand while living in Washington with his family during his father's last year in the Senate. He did not really like the law. He did not like politics. He decided to enter the Episcopal priesthood—a career his parents also approved, since his maternal grandfather had long been a Trinity vestryman, to be succeeded in the office by Morgan's father, the ambidextrous general. Morgan studied three years at the General Theological Seminary and was ordained a deacon in 1852 at St. John's Chapel, another unit of Trinity Parish—the same chapel where he had been baptized and confirmed, and where his father in 1826 had been married to Catherine Morgan. From that time on, except for a brief term as assistant minister at St. Mark's in Philadelphia, the life of Morgan Dix had been identified with Trinity Parish. He took a deep pride in supervising a parish that had ancestral ties with his family—a parish founded when New York was a city of 6,000 inhabitants, 1,500 of them Indians and slaves.

As he moved into middle age, engrossed in his ministry and speaking admiringly of celibacy, his perpetual bachelorhood seemed such a certainty that his engagement and marriage to Emily Woolsey Soutter in 1874, when he was forty-six and she twenty-three, produced something closer to shock than surprise. Typically, he kept it from the press so well that the *Herald* complained, "All the arrangements were of the most quiet nature, and nothing but the great number of elegant flowers that were carried in could attract attention." It was almost as if the rector had been discovered in delinquency. The Beecher-Tilton scandal, then dragging through the courts to the embarrassment of Plymouth Church and the delight of the newspapers, had caused a general increase in vigilance toward pastoral romance and marriage. Over the decades, the rectorship of Trinity had become surrounded by rules almost as rigid as those of the Vatican. For a holder of the office to cause surprise, much less shock, in his own matrimonial affairs, and for him to marry a woman half his age, might have been expected to get him in hot water. Morgan Dix turned the crisis into triumph simply by choosing a bride so charming that crusty, long-bearded vestrymen could hardly forbear from chucking her under the chin. Emily Dix's high intelligence and stimulating conversation came near concealing the fact that she was not really beautiful, and indeed too much feminine allure would have been suspect. As Vestryman Strong noted, she had qualities indispensable for a rector's wife, "including the agreeable gift of implying things complimentary and flattering without expressly saying them." She so impressed the vestry that it voted the rector a $5,000 extra allowance and a six-months' leave, which the couple spent in extensive European travel.

This kind of largess angered other churchmen, even of the Episcopalian persuasion, who felt that such a sum could have been better used for the poor or the propagation of the faith. The vestry, accustomed to handling large sums and accustomed also to the envy of the less affluent, had long been snootily imperturbable in the face of such criticism. As for Dr. Dix, he was worldly enough so that in London he visited the famous Poole's to order some black broadcloth suits. When Poole's representative mentioned that they could not take orders from strangers, the rector thought he had the perfect answer in proffering a letter of introduction Bishop Horatio Potter of his diocese had given him to present to the Archbishop of Canterbury. Poole's man, while venturing that this might be impressive in ecclesiastical circles, said, "It won't do here, sir." Dr. Dix got no fittings at Poole's until he returned from the City with a letter from his banker.

The fact that the new Mrs. Dix came from a Southern family only one generation in New York raised a problem for Morgan's father, the aging general, who had dedicated himself to the extermination of rebels in the late conflict and as a Cabinet member had uttered the most stirring of pre-war Union rallying cries: "If anyone attempts to haul down the American flag, shoot him on the spot!" He made it a rule never to mention the war in her presence, a nicety noticed with suppressed amusement by Emily Dix.

Shortly before his marriage, Dr. Dix had moved regretfully from the old rectory at 50 Varick Street, a place he had come to love, to new and imposing quarters at 27 West Twenty-fifth Street, a dozen doors from Broadway as it angles northward from Madison Square and next door to Trinity Chapel, an uptown appendage of his parish. The change was recommended by the vestry so that he would be more centrally located, many of Trinity's communicants having joined the uptown migration, and still another parish chapel, St. Chrysostom's, being farther yonder on Thirty-ninth Street. To this big brownstone house the rector took his bride on returning from Europe, and here their first child was born in 1878.

More central it truly was, but there were disadvantages. Famous Fifth Avenue, of course, was only a stone's throw eastward, and Twenty-fifth Street itself was a thoroughfare of high fashion and respectability for a short distance westward. Alas, the distance was all too short. Striding westward one could, in a manner of speaking, quickly descend from heaven to hell. As one approached Sixth Avenue the family homes gave way to a row of the most quietly ornate and expensive brothels in town, one of them being the well-known Seven Sisters, said to be operated by starchy siblings from New England who catered only to silk hats. Sixth Avenue itself had no silk-hat pretensions. It was the rialto of commercialized vice, the center of the burgeoning Tenderloin, with such notorious "music and entertainment" places as the Haymarket at Thirtieth Street, the Star & Garter across the way, the Bohemia and the Heart of Maryland near Twenty-ninth and a score of other clangorous sinks of debauchery, including the Cremorne and the French Madame's, nearby. The side streets were devoted to quieter deadfalls—houses of assignation, panel joints, easy-going hotels and cribs where the music might consist of a violin and piano instead of a brass band. Experts in these matters declared that the bagnios were most numerous on Thirty-fifth, Thirty-second, Thirty-first, Twenty-fourth and on the Dixes' own Twenty-fifth Street. It was common in the early-morning hours for the rector's household to be disturbed by the shrieks and shouts of roisterers both male and female passing by in carriages. When Dr. Dix drove up to St. Chrysostom's before noon he found Sixth Avenue shuttered and lifeless, its denizens sleeping off their orgies. By four o'clock it began to revive with the flow of liquor, and with every succeeding hour it became a noisier jungle of painted women and the various amusements and swindles built around them.

This condition seemed to persist whether Tammany enjoyed its usual rule or the city was gripped by one of its brief interludes of reform. The post of captain in the Tenderloin precinct was as highly prized among the police as was a directorship in a railroad or banking firm among men devoted to more prosaic pursuits. Captain Alexander "Clubber" Williams, who held the job for nine years, was able to retire to a seventeen-room mansion in Cos Cob and to sail the Sound in a luxurious fifty-three-foot yacht. Even beat men in the area expected to be treated to champagne and sizable weekly payments by madams and crooks whom they indulged. All this was as well known to Dr. Dix as to Dr. Talmage of the Brooklyn Tabernacle. Talmage had the nerve to come over from Brooklyn on repeated tours of the Tenderloin, which he christened Satan's Circus, and made it the subject of a series of sermons during which he said that if he were given two hundred honest policemen he could clean up the district in forty-eight hours. Although Dix suffered more from the Tenderloin than Talmage out of mere propinquity, he did not mount any direct pulpit attack on it. This was not for lack of courage but because of his sense of priestly dignity and his revulsion against secularity and sensationalism. He disliked to celebrate and publicize sin by pointing directly at it. True, Talmage's spicy descriptions of Tenderloin shame filled his huge tabernacle as well as his weekly "religious" column which ran in more than three hundred newspapers. To Dix, Talmage was vulgar and most of his listeners and readers morons. The rector preferred to assail evil in the abstract, not by name or street number, and while he would lament private and public looseness, he would never specifically mention the Seven Sisters, the Haymarket or Captain Williams. A dozen years later he would also disapprove of the methods of his Madison Square Presbyterian colleague, Dr. Charles H. Parkhurst, even though Parkhurst's abandonment of propriety in going into the Tenderloin disguised as a man on the town, visiting one low resort after another, drinking liquor and witnessing innumerable obscenities, actually resulted in evidence that brought a cleansing, if short, wave of civic regeneration.

One did not need to dive into the gutter to discover that it was dirty. Gutter-divers such as Talmage and Parkhurst were not above the suspicion that they derived some enjoyment from the sins they exposed and the headlines they made. And was it not true that the "reforms" achieved by these specious methods were illusory? Every municipal cleanup was in fact merely a relocation of vice. When in time the Tenderloin would be purified, it would mean simply that the brothels moved elsewhere and that other police captains would be collecting the revenues once enjoyed by Williams. This was by no means to suggest that reform was impossible—simply that the only meaningful reform lay in the human heart and soul, the acceptance of Christ that meant automatically the end of vice.

But now Dr. Dix's attention, with a self-preoccupation unusual to him, was centered not on eternal verities but on his own harassments. He found himself waiting the next move of his tormentor with a suspense unbecoming to one who has complete faith in God. He had spoken of it only in jocular terms to Emily Dix because she was expecting her second child and he wanted to protect her from additional worry.

CHAPTER III
ENTER GENTLEMAN JOE

On Monday, February twenty-third, a squally morning with a high wind blowing wet snow, the rector was still sipping his breakfast tea when he had his first caller. It was a Mrs. Zickels, clad in a threadbare overcoat and woolen shawl, who left a rickety wagon drawn by an ancient nag on the street in front as she spoke to him in heavily accented English. He gathered that she was the wife of a Chatham Street dealer in used clothing. She had come to appraise and to buy Mrs. Dix's wardrobe if the price was right. She had a postcard which she waved as if it were a ticket of admission. Of course it was the work of the same impostor, who signed Dr. Dix's name to an invitation that she look over his wife's clothing, which was to be discarded in toto because of the new spring styles.

With some difficulty the rector managed to make her understand that it was a hoax and that Mrs. Dix was not selling any clothing—a story she received skeptically, complaining that she had come a long way and evidently suspecting that she was being cheated out of what might be a profitable deal. She only begged permission to *see* the clothing, she said, declaring that she paid the best prices. Even when Dr. Dix persuaded her to leave, she repeated her claim that she paid top prices, making it evident that she did not believe a word he said.

She retired warily to stand beside her wagon in the snow, keeping the rectory under surveillance as another second-hand clothing dealer, Mrs. Lindeman, arrived. Dr. Dix, one of the most courteous of men, went through the same process with her. She was even harder to persuade, for she had no horse but only a pushcart which she indicated with her thumb as she told him of her labor in pushing it two miles uptown. Now Mrs. Zickels advanced once more, scowling in the belief that Mrs. Lindeman might be given the benefit of a deal denied her. The two women, previously acquainted as business competitors, shrieked angrily at each other. This went on all morning as other women and a few men in the same calling, all of them from the Lower East Side, arrived at regular intervals. The rector was able to coax most of them to surrender their postcards. He saw that the writer, with an eye for efficiency, had specified the exact time for each dealer to call, spacing them so that they would arrive in continuous procession. He was so anxious for accuracy in this respect that in his card to one of them, a Mrs. Weiss, he had instructed her to call at 10:30, then scratched this out and substituted 10:45.

By noon, when the snow had stopped but the wind was still strong enough to tear and dislodge some of the bunting displayed at many houses along the street, there were, according to a contemporary account, twenty-eight old-clothes dealers and a swarm of neighborhood children gathered in front of the rectory. The street was choked with wagons, pushcarts and people. Most of the dealers, feeling that Dr. Dix was deceiving them and possibly jockeying for the best price, had camped outside, waiting it out on the theory that persistence might yet win them a piece of business. Several shrill arguments broke out among them. In the midst of this, S. Appelbaum, a pawn-broker of Sixth Avenue, arrived to say that he would pay generously for the jewelry and musical instruments Dr. Dix wished to pledge but that he could pay nothing for old gold bridgework. The market for that was depressed. Thereafter, fourteen more pawnbrokers called at regular intervals, each under the impression that a hard-pressed rector had appealed to him for financial help.

Since many offices had closed to honor Washington, throngs of liberated workers had gathered along Broadway in the hope of seeing a parade that never materialized. Groups of these watchers noticed the commotion around the rectory and strolled over to join the fun. Others who swelled the assemblage—pasty-faced men in checker-board clothing, and bedizened women—obviously came from the Tenderloin. There was jeering as Dr. Dix appeared at the door to turn away yet another clothes dealer—an animus apparently inspired simply by sympathy for a poor person being rejected by a man of wealth. As the crowd grew in noise and numbers, a riot seemed a possibility on Twenty-fifth Street. Emily Dix, peering out a window, became increasingly nervous. Her husband, one of the early owners of Bell's recent invention, overcame his reluctance and telephoned police headquarters, bringing a squad of bluecoats who cleared the street. Police Chief George W. Walling, who considered the case one of the strangest in his experience, covered this phase of it in his subsequent memoirs, writing:

> The last one of these women had scarcely been driven away, and the police had hardly departed, when a carriage whirled rapidly around the corner from Fifth Avenue, stopped before the parsonage, and one of the leading physicians of the city sprang hastily out and ran up the steps. He had scarcely pulled the bell, when two more carriages came swiftly down the street and also stopped in front of the house, and two more eminent physicians hurriedly entered the house. Each one told Dr. Dix

that he had been summoned by a messenger to come directly to the parsonage, as the pastor had gone into an epileptic fit and was feared to be dying. The same summons had been sent to twenty or thirty physicians, and their visits continued until late in the evening.

Postal employees were not on holiday, so that mails were delivered. Dr. Dix went over his letters during the intervals between his coping with the doctors. His mail from heavy industries was holding up well, lightened by such new contributions as a letter from a Louisville distiller thanking him for his unsolicited testimonial about the medicinal properties of their bourbon and particularly for his permission to be quoted in their advertising; a case of their product would follow by express. A Cleveland manufacturer quoted prices on whalebone-reinforced corsets in the belief that the rector would order them wholesale for the Episcopal Sisterhood of St. Mary. An entirely new problem was posed by more than two dozen letters from Episcopal clergymen, with some of whom he was acquainted, including the Reverend Drs. Phillips Brooks of Boston, Charles Hall of Brooklyn, F. C. Fair of Baltimore and Abram Littlejohn, bishop of Long Island. Each of them wrote in stately, more-in-sorrow-than-anger tones, making it apparent that they believed Dr. Dix had addressed them in sharp criticism, demanding to know why they had not answered his previous letters. This was serious. Each would have to be written at once in careful explanation.

In the same mail was a letter that the rector studied eagerly, for it was written in the identical hand as that of the forger who had sent the hundreds of postcards in his name. Enclosed in a government-machine-stamped envelope and written on plain paper, it read:

Read this carefully—one thousand dollars will stop the racket.

Dr. Morgan Dix, D.D. Dear Sir: I was a classmate of yours in college, and thinking a good deal of you as I do, I have tried my best to put a stop to the annoyance in regard to the many letters and postal cards sent you. The gentleman who sends these means no harm, and has never been on this racket before. He professes to know all about your private affairs and says he will stop this game for a thousand dollars; as you get 25,000 a year you won't miss it much.... I offered him a hundred dollars out of my own pocket to stop it, but he wants 1,000 dollars, and says he must have it next week; if he doesn't get it he says he will expose your private character with a girl in *The New-York Sun*, which will gladly publish it—other papers will copy it. He says he will publish cards in all the papers next week asking Five Hundred people to call at your house, and I know he will do it. I will pledge my honor as a gentleman if you will pay the 1,000 dollars he will stop it—he will want it in currency—put a personal in *The Herald* exactly like I put on the opposite page—put it in Tuesday morning—and I will tell you where to send the money. I would gladly pay it myself, but I can't afford it. Always your friend, old classmate,

J. T. M.

On the opposite page was written, "Put this in personal as follows: Gentleman Joe—All right. M. D."

No matter how much he studied the missive, the rector did not know just how to take it. Its tinge of sly humor—if it *was* humor—made it hard to divine whether the demand for money was jocular or menacing. It seemed likely that J. T. M. or Gentleman Joe was himself the forger, the author of the hoax. He was wrong about the rector's salary, which was $10,000, and of course about his "private character with a girl"—a crude intimation of scandal that made the upright clergyman really angry. Aside from these vulgarities, the writing exuded a whiff of light-hearted fictitiousness, much like a fairy tale that is not expected to be believed, and which suggested that Gentleman Joe would be an exceedingly unreliable person to deal with, if indeed he intended to make any deal.

Much as Dr. Dix wanted to end his affliction, not for a moment did he consider inserting a personal message in the *Herald* or paying any money. "I thought it merely another device to annoy me," he later said. The *Herald*, which had won enormous circulation and affluence under the elder James Gordon Bennett, continued to thrive in the hands of his eccentric son and namesake. Like the latter, it had a split personality. It was preeminently the society paper of the day, giving effusive coverage to full-dress gatherings on Fifth Avenue or at Newport and faithful attention even to modest middle-class affairs in Harlem. It was read by everyone either in "society" or interested in it. On the other hand, among its many columns of classified advertisements was a Personals department often used by quacks, con men, fences and particularly by brothel madams and free-lance trollops seeking custom. Clients of "Mrs. Treadway and her attractive protégées" were informed that the troupe had left Twenty-ninth Street and could be reached until further notice at a *Herald* box number. The *Herald* was dotted with interesting invitations: "2 AMIABLE YOUNG LADIES desire the assistance of two honorable gentlemen to further their interest for the stage."

But there were factors other than the *Herald*'s raciness to consider. A corollary of the rector's detestation of publicity was his extravagant regard for his own and his family's privacy. Newspapers were professional invaders of privacy and he wanted nothing to do with them. Nor did he want any communication with anyone so scoundrelly as Gentleman Joe. Further, the bald threat of "exposing" conduct of which he was not guilty dictated caution. In his position it was required not only to maintain rectitude but also the appearance of it. If he placed the message in the *Herald* and it became known, it might be construed as an admission that he was not guiltless and was ready to deal with a blackmailer to save his reputation.

Still, as he put it, "When a fly buzzes around your head you simply brush it away; but when a whole lot of hornets surround you it is time to do something." On the morning of February twenty-fourth he took his carriage downtown to the Post Office. He laid the case before Postmaster Thomas L. James, giving him the letter from Gentleman Joe as well as all the postcards he had collected.

CHAPTER IV

MALICIOUS MONKEY TRICKS

Postmaster James called in James Gayler, the superintendent of city delivery, a former special agent who was skilled in the investigation of illegal use of the mails. Gayler had worked under Dr. Dix's father when the general, for a brief period in 1860, had served as New York City's postmaster and had endeared himself to the employees by refusing to permit the Democratic party to levy a percentage of their salaries for political use. Both officials regretted that Dr. Dix had not come to them sooner. They also regretted that the suggested personal advertisement had not been inserted in the *Herald* since it might have offered an opportunity to trap the culprit if he appointed a rendezvous for collection of the money.

Strangely, in glancing over that morning's *Herald*, they saw that Gentleman Joe was well publicized there. In the midst of a welter of arrangements for assignation were three one-line personals in a row:

Gentleman Joe—Will give $50. —S.846.
Gentleman Joe—All right. —A. S. K.
Gentleman Joe—All right. —100 5th.

Since Dr. Dix had inserted none of these, they seemed to indicate that Gentleman Joe was simultaneously shaking down other victims. But the rector still regarded him as a nuisance rather than a threat. "I don't believe that was a blackmailing letter," he said. "It was simply of a piece with the rest. The whole appears to me to be a series of malicious monkey tricks."

He was anything but a timid man. On one occasion he left St. Augustine's Chapel on East Houston Street, another of the seven churches in his parish, and boarded a carriage driven by one George McDonough who, as the *Times* put it, "was not sober." The horses, frightened by some sudden street noise, bolted up the Bowery. McDonough tried briefly to get them under control, then leaped clear for his own safety, leaving the reins trailing and the rector helpless inside the careening carriage. A crowd pursuing it with loud shouts did not quiet the horses. The carriage sideswiped another cab, losing a lamp, then grazed an elevated-railroad pillar. Luckily, a policeman at Fourth Street named Lefferts saw the horses coming, dashed alongside, seized a bridle and brought them to a halt, upon which "the Rev. Dr. Dix stepped from the coach, and appeared but little alarmed."

Probably he never doubted that God, whom he had aided for so long, would not fail to return the favor. The Post Office men, however, were unwilling to depend on the Deity to handle Gentleman Joe. Although Joe might be a mere practical joker or crank, they saw a touch of madness as well as method in his operations that made it plausible to envision him as a psychopath capable of any enormity. Nor were they forgetting the kidnaping of four-year-old Charley Ross, son of a wealthy Philadelphian, still unsolved after six years. The rector had an infant daughter. James and Gayler were distressed by his tendency to underrate the seriousness of the case, his desire to keep the police out of it and to prevent any publicity in the newspapers. They persuaded him that he needed an attorney to advise him and to serve as liaison between him and the investigators. The rector retained Colonel George Bliss, the fifty-year-old, Harvard-trained former United States Attorney who had distinguished himself in the Civil War by organizing three regiments of colored infantry, and later by drafting the New York charter of 1873, and now was among those booming General Grant for a third term as President. Dix and Bliss were good friends, both being officers of the Veteran Corps of Artillery, State of New York.

Bliss saw immediately that his friend took too light an attitude. He pointed out that Gentleman Joe's letter on its face seemed an attempt at extortion and that the safest strategy was to assume that he meant it and might be dangerous. The rector thereupon agreed that the police should be notified.

Captain Thomas Byrnes, recently appointed chief of detectives, took charge. He assigned several plainclothesmen to keep an around-the-clock watch at the Dix home against a possible kidnap attempt or other fell design. The beefy, mustachioed, thirty-eight-year-old Byrnes had won fame by solving the $2,000,000 Manhattan Savings Bank robbery in 1878, and by reorganizing the detective force, which he increased from twenty-eight to forty men. Intelligent, efficient, he was many cuts above the ruthless Clubber Williams and yet perhaps he was not averse to making occasional expedient use of his power. Indeed, it was unrealistic to expect lily-white honesty from police officers when the politicians running the city were notoriously venal. Byrnes had just opened an office at 17 Wall Street as a station for eight detectives whom he detailed to protect such stock-market operators as Jay Gould (a special Byrnes friend) not only from robbers and blackmailers but also from angry speculators who had been victimized by fast work in stocks behind the scenes. When

Byrnes was later investigated and found to have $350,000 tucked away, he swore it came from lucky investments made on stock tips given him mostly by a grateful Gould. He was allowed to resign, which did not hurt him at all, for before his death he owned a Fifth Avenue building worth $550,000 and a total fortune near a million. Now, however, he gave close attention to the Dix case, for while the force was inclined to shrug off the difficulties of the poor, the Dixes were important people.

First, those three *Herald* personals addressed to Gentleman Joe. A detective called at the *Herald* and was given the names and addresses of A. S. K., S.846 and 100 5th. A. S. K. turned out to be S. J. Levy, a well-known textile man living at the Astor House, who had lost some valuable jewelry and had advertised in the *Herald* for it. Next day, he said, he had received a postcard from a man identifying himself as "Gentleman Joe" who agreed to negotiate the return of the jewelry for a suitable reward if the owner would place a personal in Monday's *Herald* reading, "Gentleman Joe—All right." Levy had merely complied and was now waiting further word from Joe. He still had Joe's postcard. The detective had that feeling of impending triumph known only to the successful gumshoe when he recognized the script as that of the same Gentleman Joe who was annoying Dr. Dix. He asked Levy to follow precisely the instructions he would doubtless receive from Gentleman Joe. If the latter suggested a meeting, Levy was to notify the detective bureau so that investigators could be at the scene.

The other two men turned out to have lost a fur coat and a half-carat-diamond stickpin respectively. They had also advertised for the lost articles, and also had received postcards from Joe. These two were given the same instructions. It seemed clear that the items that the trio had lost had actually been stolen, and that Gentleman Joe, in addition to being a blackmailer and extortionist, was one of the city's most active fences.

Although it seemed preposterous to think that Joe could also be an "old classmate" of the rector's, as he claimed, the point was checked out. Morgan Dix had graduated at the head of his class, a member of Phi Beta Kappa. He had spoken his valedictory in Greek before lumpily dressed women who applauded him without the slightest suspicion that his address was a satire on ladies' fashions of the day. Columbia was then so small that the class numbered less than forty, all, of course, men. None had the initials J. T. M., but almost a score of them were business or professional men still in the New York area thirty-two years after commencement. True, Dix could not recall a single enemy among them, and in fact some were still his good friends. Nevertheless, a quiet investigation was begun of the class of 1848, as well as his subsequent classmates at the General Theological Seminary. So far, although publicity would have served to put the public on guard against the bogus letters, not a word about the affair had appeared in the newspapers. The secrecy was now continued in order to spare the rector embarrassment and to relieve the pregnant Emily Dix of excessive worry.

Weird crimes had not been uncommon during this period of business depression, and another one even more gothic in atmosphere was still being investigated by Byrnes' men. The body of the late merchant multimillionaire, A. T. Stewart, had been stolen from its huge churchyard vault at St. Mark's-in-the-Bouwerie at Second Avenue and Tenth Street. Why anyone should want bones which had been underground for thirty months became plain when Stewart's aged widow received letters demanding $25,000 for their return. Her agent was still dickering with the criminals, who would ultimately get $20,000 for surrendering the remains in a lonely spot in Westchester. Dr. Dix had heard the details from his friend, Dr. Joseph Rylance, rector of St. Mark's. He had had immediate qualms about the safety of hallowed graves such as Alexander Hamilton's, Robert Fulton's and Albert Gallatin's in Trinity's old churchyard, and sextons had since kept a nightly watch there. The police explored the possibility that the body snatcher and Gentleman Joe might be the same, but thought it unlikely because the phraseology of the two culprits was as different as the handwriting, Joe's letters exhibiting a fluency and imagination entirely lacking in those of the graveyard despoiler.

Colonel Bliss spent hours with Dr. Dix, going over both his personal and professional background in the hope of turning up some quarrel, enmity or jealousy that might furnish a clue.

"I can think of no one, clerical or lay," the rector said, "who could have the slightest provocation for attempting such a thing, and yet it seems hardly possible that a perfect stranger would have undertaken it. The style of writing, the choice of language, the thorough acquaintance with the titles and residences of bishops and clergymen and the wholesale and persistent way in which the work is carried on would seem to indicate that the author is a person of leisure and some means, and, moreover, pretty thoroughly versed in church affairs."

CHAPTER V

OLD IRELAND FOREVER!

As Superintendent Gayler and a corps of postal men began sorting and scrutinizing the postcards in an effort to find some intimation of the forger's identity, the baneful campaign persisted. On February twenty-fourth, the same morning that Dix called for help, a parade of shoe dealers, most of them from Fourteenth Street, called at the rectory in response to postcards requesting them to submit bids for fitting a whole regiment of poor children of the parish. Each of them brought samples of the "sturdy rather than stylish" shoes the post-cards designated, both for boys and girls. Like the used-clothing dealers, they had been asked to call at specific times so that they arrived in a continuous procession. At luncheon time, while servants were still turning away the shoe men and collecting their postcards, a number of the clergy began to arrive, all of them exhibiting the greatest pleasure and anticipation. It turned out that each of the priests had received postcards reading:

> Mrs. Dr. Dix would be pleased to have the company of the Rev. Dr. ———— at luncheon on Tuesday, February 24, at 1:30, to meet the Bishop of Exeter, England.

There was a small discrepancy here, some of the cards saying it was the bishop of York who would be honored, but the callers were as eager for York as for Exeter. Dr. Dix, back from the Post Office, was so touched at their disappointment when he told them of the hoax that he felt the least he could do was to invite them—fourteen of them—for tea. Other ministers receiving the same invitation had been less credulous, among them the Reverend Dr. Herman Dyer, assistant rector of the Church of the Ascension on Fifth Avenue.

"I saw at once that it was bogus," Dr. Dyer said later. "Ladies like Mrs. Dix are not in the habit of sending invitations to lunch on postal cards." He mailed the card back to the Dixes along with a humorous note saying he was desolated at being unable to meet the English bishop.

Dr. Rylance of St. Mark's—the same whose churchyard had been robbed of Stewart's body—had also received an invitation. He paid particular attention to his grooming and was about to leave when his wife examined the postcard and said firmly that Mrs. Dix would never have sent such a message on anything but the creamiest notepaper enclosed in an envelope. Dr. Rylance agreed and hung up his hat. He was startled that same day to receive a letter purportedly from his brother, starting off impulsively, "My Dear Joe: By the time you read this I shall be no more—I have deliberately decided to commit suicide," and, after mournfully recounting the "misfortune in Berlin" leading to the decision, bidding farewell with the signature, "Your Brother, Will Rylance."

Dr. Rylance was less concerned than he might have been because his only brother was not named Will, had never been in Berlin and had a hand totally unlike this. He noted that the handwriting was the same as that on the "Mrs. Dr. Dix" postcard, and kept both missives as souvenirs of human eccentricity. That same day, Lord & Taylor, Stern Brothers, Tiffany's, A. T. Stewart & Company, Arnold Constable and a dozen other stores enjoying the Dix custom reacted nervously on receiving cards signed in the rector's name, telling them their insulting letters had been turned over to counsel who would proceed against them to the limit of the law. They hastened to write assurances that they had the highest respect for him and had sent no such letters.

That afternoon, an angry-looking gentleman who carried a walking stick as if it were a bludgeon, brushed aside a servant at the rectory door and dashed into the sitting room to confront Dr. Dix. According to Police Chief Walling's possibly embroidered account, he shouted, "You lecherous old hypocrite! You're a fine plum for a minister of the gospel, you are—you sniffling, sanctimonious old sinner!"

It transpired that his wife had received a letter proposing a romantic rendezvous with the rector. Endearingly phrased, it urged that they meet outside the lobby of Daly's New Theater at Broadway and Thirtieth Street and then repair to a snug little hideout he knew of where they could enjoy perfect privacy. Dr. Dix had to talk with quick eloquence and display the bogus missives he had received that day to subdue his caller's rage and send him away without violence. His secular mail had dwindled, containing only a dozen-odd letters from deluded manufacturers, which were funneled to his secretary in what had become an efficient routine. There was one letter from another angry husband who accused Dr. Dix of proposing a meeting with the former's wife at Tony Pastor's on Broadway and demanding an explanation before the matter was referred to an attorney—a problem the rector quickly handled through his own attorney.

The next day, Wednesday, February twenty-fifth, the trickle slowed to a driblet—only one letter connected with the deception, but one that seemed of surpassing importance. It was a short note from Gentleman Joe himself saying that his friend was still expecting the $1,000 and that if the rector was ready to pay he could negotiate with D. Buckley, of 30 Third Avenue. Dix gave the letter to Colonel Bliss, who showed his excitement at the rascal's first obvious blunder and immediately passed the note to the police. Captain Byrnes, too, was elated. He became downright jubilant when he heard that same morning from Levy and the other two who had advertised for their lost property. The three of them had received identical postcards, reading:

> Call at D. Buckley's saloon, No. 30 Third-ave., at 5 o'clock Wednesday afternoon, and no other time. Bring the money with you, and receive the goods. No humbug with me, if you please.
>
> Gentleman Joe

This was one of those rare moments detectives live for—the equivalent in sleuthing of the inventor suddenly hitting on the idea that makes his contrivance work, or the scholar finding the long-sought missing manuscript. Joe was a bungler after all, walking straight into the trap. How wonderful, and at the same time, how amusing! Sometimes, even with the cleverest of rogues, one only had to give him a little rope and he would hang himself.

Still, Byrnes was not one to tip his hand prematurely. He sent men to make undercover inquiries about Buckley, who of course must be Gentleman Joe. They found him to be Daniel Buckley, a red-faced, middle-aged barrelhouse proprietor at Third Avenue and Ninth Street, who lived with his wife and children above the drinkery. He had no police record. He was regarded in the neighborhood as respectable. He was an Irish Catholic, which might conceivably cause him to combine the pleasure of badgering an Episcopal clergyman with the business of extorting money from him.

Byrnes gave careful instructions to Levy and the other two. They were to keep the five o'clock appointment at the saloon. They were to pay Buckley with marked bills that would serve as evidence against him. Then they were to leave quietly with their recovered property and meet Byrnes and his men, who would be waiting at the next corner and who would then close in for the arrest.

The three enacted their roles to perfection. They arrived at the saloon around 5:00, separately. But by 5:20 they were conferring in puzzlement with the investigators on the Eighth Street corner. The thing had not gone according to script. Buckley, obviously in a bad humor, had not turned over the stolen goods. He had put on an honest front, claiming that he was the victim of an error and that he was decidedly not Gentleman Joe. The three were of the opinion that in some way he must have divined his danger.

Byrnes was deeply disappointed. The conclusive, open-and-shut evidence he expected had been denied him, and he gave the matter careful thought. At length he decided that they must make the pinch nevertheless. After all, the circumstantial evidence against Buckley was strong, and all they needed to cinch it was proof that his handwriting was the same as Joe's. They entered the saloon to find it filled with convivial Irishmen. Buckley, however, had gone, leaving his helper in charge. When he returned a half-hour later, two detectives cornered him behind the bar and fired questions at him while two others pawed through bills and invoices to find samples of the Buckley handwriting.

Disappointingly, his rough hen-track scrawl bore no resemblance to the forger's elegant script. Buckley's own reaction to the arrest was violent. He purpled, swelled in anger and uttered a string of imprecations that seemed directed more at a malign fate than at the detectives. After he had recovered his composure he told a long story which his listeners took in skeptically, for he claimed to be another sufferer at the hands of Gentleman Joe rather than the culprit himself.

Odd things had been happening to him too, Buckley said. They began on the previous Saturday, February twenty-first, when strangers speaking with the rich flavor of Mayo and Roscommon streamed into his bar as though on holiday and ordered up. They asked if he was Mr. Buckley. They shook his hand, complimented him on his great Irish heart and declared that in such a cause a man had the purest of motives for getting a little mellow, even if there were bills to be paid and the old woman was snorting like a dragon. Puzzled, Buckley discovered that they believed he had made some sort of patriotic announcement in the *Herald*. Looking into that morning's issue, he saw the following letter under the heading, "A Bar Offer":

To The Editor of The Herald:—

I will devote every cent received at my bar on Saturday, the 21st inst., day and night, for the benefit of the Irish Relief Fund, and will send you the amount on Monday morning.

D. Buckley
Corner of Third avenue and Ninth street

The failure of potatoes and other crops had again caused appalling privation in western Ireland, inducing the *Herald*, not without a canny eye for circulation among New York's throngs of Irish-born, to inaugurate a relief fund which had already gathered upwards of $200,000. It was a praiseworthy effort, Buckley agreed, which he favored with all his heart. The thing that annoyed him was that he had written no such letter. Angry at the *Herald* for what he took to be a fast trick to dragoon him into contributing, he was yet unwilling to dampen the ardor of these glowing countrymen by telling them that their enthusiasm about him was unfounded and that he could not afford such liberality. To do so would probably be to send them a block north to McGroarty's saloon. Instead, he hurriedly hung up a sign written in an illegible scrawl in a far corner behind a door, informing patrons that the announcement was erroneous, so that he would not be taking money under false pretenses. He left his barman in charge while he went to the newspaper's office at Broadway and Ann Street to complain. There he was shown a postcard, written in a bold and flowing hand, with the identical message printed in the paper and signed in his name. When he disavowed the card, the *Herald* clerks thought it must be a practical joke played by some wag-gish friend. Indeed they seemed more amused than concerned, appar-ently taking the attitude that it would be a fine thing if he *did* donate the day's receipts to the fund. Commandeering the bogus postcard, he returned to his saloon to find that the wind was not entirely ill, for despite his placard attempt to make his position as clear as potheen, it had gone unnoticed, the place was crowded with men from the bogs and he did a rushing business far into the night. On the following Monday he received a letter in which the *Herald* "bar offer" had been clipped and pasted on a piece of paper and under it written:

> All honor to Buckley! Old Ireland forever! Hurrah!
> —St. Patrick and St. Bridget

That same day, James Boden, a leather merchant at 67 Eighth Avenue, received a postcard that made him boil:

> Dear Sir: You will please call immediately and settle that little bill for whiskey, &c. I have some bills to pay, and must have money. If you do not settle by Wednesday, I shall take summary measures to compel you. It's only $29.
> —D. Buckley, 30 Third Ave.

One thing that aroused Boden was that he had never heard of Buckley before, much less owing him money. Another was that the dun was written on a postcard so that all the world could read it and pass around the gossip that might give him, a respected business man, a reputation as a tosspot who left behind him a trail of unpaid bar bills. Boden dashed off a note to Buckley, saying in part:

> ...As you don't know me, and as I never was within the doors of your saloon, it looks very much as though you were trying to blackmail me.

When Buckley received this letter on February twenty-fourth, he suspected the boggards, for he had not written Boden. Also, he had just sent back four barrels of beer, ten boxes of pretzels and six cases of Irish whiskey someone had falsely ordered from the wholesaler in his name. He hurried over to Eighth Avenue and explained matters to Boden, who took it in good stead when he learned that Buckley seemed more imposed upon than he. He gave Buckley the dunning card, which was written in the same attractive hand as the one sent to the *Herald*.

At the same time, even more ominous forces were moving against Buckley. Mayor Edward Graham of Paterson, New Jersey, had just received a postcard that propelled him suddenly from his swivel chair:

> Your honor, a man who lives on the corner 3d Avenue and 9th St. New York named D. Buckley might tell you somethin about the murder of the woman, he talked pretty free of it while he was drinkin last night.
>
> A honest Mechannick who
don't want to be known

Paterson was in excitement over the murder of an attractive, flirtatious widow, thirty-year-old Mrs. Harriet Hink, who had been found in her bed on February twenty-first, her skull crushed. Mrs. Hink recently had sold her late husband's farm near Port Jervis, New

York, and taken lodgings at the home of Mrs. Martha Sneeden at Bridge and Division Streets in Paterson. She talked of buying and operating a restaurant, and was rather free in flashing a large roll of currency paid her for the farm. On the night of the murder, Mrs. Sneeden had heard Mrs. Hink on the floor below in conversation with a man she described as speaking with an Irish brogue. On Mrs. Hink's body, when it was found the next day, lay a shotgun. Old and rust-caked, it had not been fired in years but obviously had been left by the killer in an effort to beguile the authorities into writing off the case as a suicide. The murder actually had been committed with an axe, found in a corner, which still bore traces of blood although the killer had tried to scour the blade with ashes from the stove. The widow's money had disappeared—all but forty cents in change—as had a valuable gold watch she had worn. The case had been provocative enough to get splash attention in the New York papers.

Mayor Graham, who would be up for reelection that year, evidently felt that his own participation in a swift solution of the mystery would do him no harm at the polls. He grabbed his police chief and the two men ferried over to Manhattan, took a carriage to the saloon and, according to a subsequent account in the *Times*, "taking Mr. Buckley into his private office, endeavored to extort from him a confession that he was the murderer of the woman." Buckley, who had come as a young man from Limerick, had the inevitable brogue and was in deep trouble for a while. The police chief began a search of the premises for the missing gold watch while the mayor continued the questioning. Buckley finally established his innocence by proving that he had been in New York at the time of the murder, and gave evidence of the hoax by showing the officials the postcards forged in his name and sent to the *Herald* and to Boden.

The Paterson men brought out the postcard from the "honest Mechannick," which, it seemed plain, was written by the same hand. They apologized, surrendered the postcard and returned to

Jersey, leaving Buckley in need of some of his own restoratives. He took several restoratives. Around five o'clock, when he was feeling somewhat better, a well-dressed stranger entered the saloon with a rather furtive air, approached Buckley and said in a whisper, "I am S.846." This, of course, was one of the men who had advertised for his lost property. According to the *Times* account, "Mr. Buckley at this time was disgusted with the mystery which surrounded him, and exclaimed somewhat irritably, 'The ———— you say! Well, what do you want?' "

The man, unnerved by the hostile reception, went into guarded explanations which at first meant nothing to the saloonkeeper. At length, however, he began to comprehend the situation. S.846 produced the postcard from Gentleman Joe and showed it to Buckley, who was sure that the handwriting was the same as in the other bogus cards. As they parleyed, another stranger entered and spoke to Buckley in a low tone, asking, "Where is Joe?" He was followed by a third, likewise asking for Gentleman Joe. There was a good deal of palaver among the four. Buckley earnestly insisted that he knew nothing about any lost fur coats and jewelry and he knew nothing about Gentleman Joe but would like to get his hands on him. After the three men left, Buckley finally had time to look at his mail. He found a postcard from James Boden that staggered him:

> Since I saw you I have received another impertinent postal card, and I am now satisfied that you are the author. I am going to sue you for $15,000 damages. The next time you hear from me it will be through the Supreme Court.
>
> —James Boden

Buckley left on the run and grabbed a carriage for Boden's place. He was well on the way when another thought smote him. He examined the postcard more closely. Although an effort had been made to

THE RECTOR AND THE ROGUE

disguise the handwriting, he was now certain that it was the work of that unspeakable destroyer of all tranquility, Gentleman Joe. Returning, he was moved to an understandable lapse of patience when he was collared in his own saloon and, for the second time within a few hours, treated with the contempt and insult reserved for criminals.

All this, of course, was Buckley's story. Having heard it and examined the postcards, Byrnes and his men gradually came to the opinion that he seemed to be telling the truth. Buckley, it appeared, was a victim, not a malefactor. But if his account cleared up a few puzzles, it created others. Why, for example, should Gentleman Joe have animus toward two such disparate persons as the rector of Trinity Parish and a Third Avenue saloonkeeper? And why, if Joe really wanted that $1,000, had he sent Dr. Dix on what would have been a wild goose chase—to negotiate with Buckley? Some of the evidence actually seemed to suggest that the hoaxer's motive was amusement rather than profit, although cynical policemen could not be expected to give credence to such a romantic theory. Nevertheless, despite the mischief Joe had caused, they could scarcely repress some admiration for the broad sweep of imagination displayed by the culprit who, working with the humblest of weapons, penny postcards, succeeded in throwing confusion into the nation's manufacturers, confounding the used-clothing dealers of the Lower East Side, and embracing in his intricate design subjects as seemingly remote as the Irish famine, epileptic fits, a murder in Paterson and the bishops of York and Exeter, to name only a few.

CHAPTER VI

FOLLOW THAT CHOIRMASTER!

At the Post Office, Superintendent Gayler added the postcards collected from Buckley and the three gentlemen who had advertised for lost property to those already supplied by Dr. Dix. Gayler relied on several veteran employees who had attained skill in recognizing penmanship characteristics through years of experience. They agreed that the Buckley and Dix collections had been written by the same person, certainly a man. The "honest Mechannick" card to the mayor of Paterson was in the same hand, with words purposely misspelled, it was reasoned, to simulate the efforts of an unlettered workman. The writing was consistently hasty, with final letters or syllables often slurred, as would be expected of a person who had dashed off hundreds of missives within a week. It did not have the studied uniformity of a clerk or bookkeeper's script. The phraseology, apt and often felicitous, made it clear that Gentleman Joe was intelligent and well educated, probably a professional man.

While there was agreement on these technicalities, opinions

differed on the cardinal question, the penman's motive. The longest of his messages—the "old classmate" letter to Dr. Dix requesting $1,000—came in for close scrutiny. His ambiguity, tongue-in-cheekery and love of hyperbole gave rise to at least four conflicting theories:

Joe was simply enjoying a huge practical joke.

He was too industrious to be joking, and was masking menace with a false jocularity.

He was a drunken prankster (a theory abetted by the saloon angle), with a bottle of ink on one side of him and a bottle of liquor on the other.

He was *not* drunk—too steadfast of purpose and accurate in detail for that—so he must be a maniac.

No one could fail to be impressed by his monastic dedication to his task, for obviously he had spent many of his wakeful hours for a week planning his strategy and writing messages. There was speculation that his sortie against Buckley, accomplished with the dispatch of hardly more than a dozen postcards, was a red herring dragged across the trail to divert investigators from his real intention, the harassment and blackmailing of Dr. Dix.

Buckley said darkly, "I have my suspicions of somebody, and he doesn't live twenty miles from here." He named as a suspect a former friend, who was questioned and cleared. February twenty-sixth must have seemed blessed to both the saloonkeeper and the clergyman, for the letters and calls each of them received that day were entirely sane, concerning matters that made sense. The investigation nevertheless went on at full speed, on the theory that Joe was only giving a temporary rest to a cramped and callused writing hand.

Dr. Dix's "old classmates" had been the subject of considerable inquiry that seemed to establish their innocence, and Colonel Bliss was again urging him to rack his memory for possible enemies. "Of course," he said, "I can think of fifty persons who might, under conceivable circumstances, attempt something of the sort." But when he was pressed it came down to only a half-dozen persons whom he could, even by straining his judgment, consider as possible suspects. Among them were a clerk in a law office that had engaged in litigation against Trinity Church, a Sunday-school teacher who had resigned in anger because of his disagreement with the teaching program and an assistant choirmaster at one of the chapels who had quarreled about the music repertoire and had ultimately been discharged. The rector, who had a strong vein of loyalty, flatly refused to permit even the mention of suspicion against any of his fourteen assistant ministers, though some were older than he, might conceivably be jealous and would, of course, have the churchly knowledge shown by Joe.

Postal clerks, armed with facsimiles of Joe's postcards, were busy at Trinity Church and all six of its chapels, examining the files of incoming mail to see if that handwriting was duplicated. Gayler and his men listed the postmarks on Joe's communications and found that, far from dumping them all into one mailbox, he had mailed them from many different boxes coming within the jurisdiction of six New York City postal stations—C, D, E, F, G and H. Some of these stations were on the East Side, some on the West, Fifth Avenue being the dividing line. Gayler reasoned that the only way the penman could have accomplished this without extensive urban travel was by starting up Fifth Avenue at Fourteenth Street, probably by carriage, and stopping at intervals to drop mail first on one side of the avenue and then the other, until he reached Fifty-ninth Street.

It was thought that such an unusual method of mailing should have been noticed. Cabbies who worked the avenue were questioned, but none could remember carrying a passenger who had stopped frequently to mail postcards. On Gayler's advice, off-duty postmen and detectives were equipped with mailbox keys and facsimiles of Joe's inimitable hand and stationed at every Fifth Avenue box between Fourteenth and Fifty-ninth Streets. They had orders to scrutinize every person who mailed postcards, open the box immediately and, if Joe's handiwork was found, arrest the mailer. The assignment proved a difficult one requiring speed with key, eye and foot. It resulted only in the questioning of several indignant citizens who quickly proved their guiltlessness.

The innocence of the law clerk was established, and suspicion now turned toward a man identified only as "a clergyman formerly connected with Trinity Parish." Specimens of this man's handwriting had been obtained and found to have no resemblance to the forger's, but it was thought that he might have an accomplice who did the writing for him. He was trailed by detectives wherever he went, including one trip to Hoboken and one to Boston. The Reverend Dr. Cornelius Swope, a good friend of Dr. Dix and assistant pastor of Trinity Chapel next door to the rectory, now produced a bogus though harmless postcard which had been sent to him from Cincinnati the previous May. This also proved to have been written by Gentleman Joe. When inquiries disclosed that a convention of musicians had been held in Cincinnati in May, and it was recalled that the choirmaster suspect had attended the convention, a detective was sent to Cincinnati to sniff out the man's movements there. But this and other leads languished or died entirely. New Yorkers in general still knew nothing about the case, despite the advice of Drs. McKim, Dyer and others privy to it that publicity would not only prevent people from being hoodwinked by fraudulent letters but might also turn up some clue to the writer's identity.

The investigators were aware of this, and some of them wanted to give the story to the press, but it appears that they deferred to Dix's continued wish for secrecy. He doubtless shrank from the burlesque some of the less scrupulous newspapers might make of his plight.

Worse yet, they might suggest or leave the inference that there was some truth in Gentleman Joe's insinuation about his "private character with a girl." Mrs. Dix was now in a highly nervous condition as a result of the week-long tumult and the talk of a possible kidnap attempt or other violence. To invite a swarm of reporters seeking interviews would hardly restore her peace of mind, nor would it help her husband to catch up with his work, which was now in some chaos.

One lamentable effect of the effort at secrecy, as was learned later, was a wave of uncertainty and ill-feeling among church and parish functionaries. The spectacle of strange clerks going through Trinity mail naturally aroused curiosity. Too many postmen, detectives and clergymen knew of the Dix *bizarrerie* to keep it quiet for long. As fragments of the story began to leak out, staff members who had not been officially informed of the facts were wounded by this seeming lack of faith in them. Some even felt that it meant they were suspected. The situation was not unlike that at a bank whose president has discovered embezzlement and begins an unannounced investigation of his employees. All seven of Trinity's churches became charged with an atmosphere of uneasiness and suspicion. Organists, deacons and vestrymen who passed in nave or transept threw narrow-eyed glances at each other that would have been more appropriate at a police precinct station or at the Tombs. Behind leaded glass and oaken doors there were furtive conversations between A and B, speculating whether C—or possibly D—might be the guilty party.

The public read nothing about this. It read instead about Stanley's third expedition in Africa, the graduation of one hundred and forty-two young doctors from Bellevue Hospital Medical College to the tune of an orchestra under Leopold Damrosch, the completion of the new Metropolitan Museum in Central Park, and the hopeful estimate of Mayor Edward Cooper that the Brooklyn Bridge (known then as the East River Bridge) would be finished in a year. It read of the near-disaster at the Madison Square Theater on Twenty-fourth

Street, a block south of the Dix residence. A workman lighted the rows of gas jets as always by using a lighted candle at the end of a long pole. When he moved on to the footlight jets he became a bit careless and instantly the $3,000 hand-embroidered silk curtain was in flames. But firemen put out the blaze and a sooty-smelling *Hazel Kirke* went on nevertheless. It read of the arrival in New York of Count Ferdinand de Lesseps, the great French engineer who had triumphed over Suez and was planning a new canal through the Isthmus of Panama. De Lesseps and his entourage put up at the luxurious Windsor Hotel at Fifth Avenue and Forty-sixth Street, where the bachelor Andrew Carnegie was spending the winter with his widowed mother. The Frenchman, aware of a strong American opposition to "foreigners" meddling in Panama, bubbled with good humor and salesmanship as he was escorted by a committee of the American Society of Civil Engineers on a tour of the city's points of interest, including the site for Bartholdi's statue of Liberty on Bedloe's Island and the newly completed Second Avenue elevated railroad.

By March second, Dr. Dix had enjoyed a full week of emancipation from forged messages and deluded visitors, and it appeared that Gentleman Joe must have turned his energies in other directions. Peace had also come to Daniel Buckley. That evening the rector journeyed to the New-York Historical Society at Second Avenue and Eleventh Street to witness the presentation to the society of a portrait of his late father, a gift of the eminent lawyer Charles O'Conor, an old friend. A select gathering including Cyrus Field, Frederick De Peyster and the Reverend Dr. Samuel Osgood heard O'Conor eulogize the general and got their first glimpse of the portrait, done by Daniel Huntington and showing General Dix as governor of the state, holding an official paper but with his unsheathed sword on a table at his side. It was a nostalgic occasion for the rector, who was even then working on his father's memoirs, in which the Huntington portrait would be one of the illustrations.

What with so many people knowing of the forgeries, it was a wonder that it was not until March thirteenth that the story broke in the *Times*, to be followed excitedly by every other newspaper. Immediately the rector, District Attorney Benjamin K. Phelps and other persons involved were besieged by reporters seeking the lowdown on a topic which, if it lacked the importance of the coming presidential election, had ten times more novelty and interest. The press burst out with long, detailed accounts of the case that brought it up-to-date from the beginning, for of course any further thought of official secrecy was abandoned. "There is one peculiarity," said the *Sun*, "that puzzles the Rev. Dr. Dix more than any other, and that is the evident knowledge of the affairs of Trinity Parish that must be possessed by the perpetrator." The *Times* commented on "his evident education and intelligence," the *World* on "the great care and system which he has exercised over his amazing deceptions," and the *Herald* on "the remarkable skill which it must be admitted he demonstrates." The *Tribune* agreed that all the evidence indicated that the annoyer of Dix and Buckley was the same man, whereas the *Evening Post* said any such idea was nonsense: "The attacks on Mr. Buckley have been made later, exhibit a different mentality, and can scarcely, to our minds, have been made by the same individual."

Dr. Dix gave interviews with good grace but there was a deplorable collapse of liaison between him and District Attorney Phelps. The district attorney reasoned that the culprit might come out of hiding or at least grow careless if he thought himself beyond the law. Phelps therefore withheld from the press the letter in which Gentleman Joe had asked for money and had talked of publicizing the rector's "private character with a girl." Then he laid a trap with a public statement containing a strategic prevarication. He said that he much regretted that he was powerless to punish Joe because the man's misdoings were so grotesque that no one had ever thought of enacting laws against them. "None of the statutes," Phelps said, "covers the offense of the writer of the Dix communications." The *Post* editorialized indignantly:

> The late freakish and malignant attacks upon the peace and comfort of the Rev. Dr. Morgan Dix suggests with force the need for certain legal provisions that do not now exist.... Even if the assailant of Dr. Dix should be discovered, he could not legally be punished. The statutes do not cover the offences of which this despicable plotter has been guilty.

Alas for Phelps' intrigue! Dr. Dix ruined it with a statement in the same papers in which the district attorney mourned his helplessness: "With all his cunning, however, [the forger] has put himself within the meshes of the law, for, though he cannot be prosecuted for black-mail, he can be for trespass and libel."

Indeed he could, and if Gentleman Joe (obviously an inveterate reader of newspapers) had not known it before, he knew it now. The press in general was of two minds about the case, deploring it in pious editorials but printing many columns of zestful copy about it in the news sections, implying journalistic gratitude to Joe for brightening their pages. To hard-bitten newspapermen, dignity was always a questionable posture. Anyone who could puncture it, as in the case of Dr. Dix, the mayor of Paterson and a few others, merited approval. One who could deflate it with the added ingredients of amusement and mystery was nothing less than a public benefactor. The Dix affair contained a timeless element of comedy—the surprise assault of the mundane and ridiculous on pride and aristocracy. Daniel Buckley, however, was a plain, forthright individual who never stood on dignity. The comedy in his case was of a different recipe but tasty in its own way—the practical man suddenly confounded by anarchy. The operations of Gentleman Joe gave newspaper readers the equivalent of a multi-ringed circus, or a show at Tony Pastor's followed by one at Harrigan & Hart's *Theatre Comique*.

CHAPTER VII

SUBTLETIES OF JOKESMANSHIP

The *Tribune*, though admitting that Joe was a skillful practitioner, pointed out that he could not claim to have originated this rarefaction of the hoax. Credit for this was given to Theodore Edward Hook, who in 1810 had worked off a grudge against Mrs. Octavia Tottenham, a wealthy and influential London widow living at 54 Berners Street in the West End, in a similar manner. Hook, a poet, playwright, novelist and wit, had already won renown as a practical joker. This coup, staged when he was twenty-two, was regarded as the crown and consummation of his work. He had all the hallmarks of talent, including an insistence on perfection of detail and a willingness to work for it. Hook and two accomplices—a Drury Lane actress and an unregenerate Oxonian—spent six weeks in writing letters to tradesmen, professional people and even peers of the realm. The letters, all mailed at the same time, purported to be orders, appointments or invitations from Mrs. Tottenham. They all named the same day and specified the hour at which the calls were to be made.

Mrs. Tottenham had a busy day. At 5 A.M. a platoon of chimney sweeps were at the door, followed by fifteen loaded coal vans, a dozen beer wagons, and conveyances carrying provisions, chinaware, musical instruments, etc. From then on there was a continuous parade of bakers bringing wedding cakes and cranberry tarts, tailors with suits of clothes, van-loads of furniture, jewelers with gems and clergy for the dying. At noon forty fishmongers arrived, each bearing cod and lobster, along with forty butchers who brought legs of mutton. In the afternoon, hundreds of fashionable people came in answer to invitations to tea, intermixed with lawyers summoned to protect the lady's interests, barbers with wigs, mantua-makers with bandboxes, dentists ready to draw teeth, *accoucheurs* and a host of others.

Hook and his confederates had taken a room across the way to see the fun. Since Berners Street was a cul-de-sac, the disorder was extreme. The Lord Mayor and his chaplain arrived, lured by a cunning Hook letter asking them to hear "the death-bed confession of a peculating Common-councilman." The governor of the Bank of England came with his entourage to hear revelations of a complicated system of fraud in his organization. The governor of the East India Company appeared for a similar reason. The Duke of Gloucester and his equerry fought their way through crowds in haste to receive a communication from "a dying woman who was formerly confidential attendant to the duke's mother." The rage of these and other important people was considerable. The London *Morning Post* said, "The officers were immediately ordered out to keep order, but it was impossible. Every officer that could be mustered was enlisted to disperse the people, and they were placed at the corners of Berners-street to try to prevent trades-people from advancing toward the house with goods."

Mrs. Tottenham had long since swooned and was under the care, not of her own physician, who could not reach the place because of the crush, but of one of the many midwives falsely summoned. The day had been planned with such generalship that tradesfolk and others came from remote parts of London—Wapping, Lambeth, White-chapel, Paddington and points between—heading for their point of convergence like lemmings swarming to their doom. Not only Berners Street was choked but every contiguous avenue, including Oxford Street, for many blocks. The roaring and cursing of draymen was heard all the day through. Business people, employees, shoppers and householders were attracted by curiosity, so that commerce was virtually suspended and pickpockets had a field day in the throng. Indeed, the economic injury in the way of lost production, theft and damage could hardly be estimated. As one account said, "There had been an awful smashing of glass, china, harpsichords, and coach-panels. Many a horse fell, never to rise again. Beer-barrels and wine-barrels had been overturned and exhausted with impunity amidst the press of countless multitudes, and drunkenness was a problem."

Yet regardless of inconvenience and damage, the public appreciation of practical jokes seemed timeless. Londoners had taken as much enjoyment in the Berners Street hoax, as it was called (Hook's authorship not being known for years), as New Yorkers did seventy years later in the Twenty-fifth Street mystery. The London news-papers exhibited an identical dichotomy, demanding the unknown miscreant's head in one breath and betraying amusement and admiration in the next. The *Tribune*'s mention of Theodore Hook's exploit caused widespread comment among newspaper readers as to the relative skill of Hook and Gentleman Joe. One reader wrote in to say that a few years after the late war, rich Mrs. Harrison Grey Otis of Boston was similarly victimized when an estimated 3,000 visitors stormed her Beacon Street home in response to invitations to a reception forged by a jokester who was never identified.

It was generally agreed that the Otis caper would have seemed a triumph of waggery, had not one read of the other two, both of which clearly excelled it in scope and execution. The palm obviously should go to Hook or Joe. Both were men of intellect and cultivation—

qualities which added an extra dimension to their work. Some felt that the pair were in a dead heat but that Hook deserved the greater honor because he was the originator (as he told his friends after the hue and cry had safely subsided). He had invented the idea just as surely as Shakespeare had invented Hamlet, and it had to be admitted that he caused far more chaos on Berners Street than Joe did on Twenty-fifth. Still, there were subtle distinctions between the two that had to be weighed with care. Anglophobia and chauvinism were factors working in Joe's favor. There were not a few New Yorkers who felt that in this case the pupil had excelled the master. Practical jokes of such depth and complexity had to be judged on a basis of points won or lost in the many levels of their planning and performance. Joe surely deserved points because he had maneuvered his forces so that no damage had been done except to complacency and order. More points were due him because he had (as the handwriting evidence made clear) been alone in producing and directing the Dix extravaganza, whereas Hook had needed two helpers. Hook had shot his bolt in one long, long day whereas Joe had kept *his* game going for a week, with no assurance that it was yet ended.

There was enough interest in Hook so that book dealers noticed a sudden burst of requests for his novels. For years they had been as dead as Plautus, gathering dust on the shelves. They had wound up at the used-book dealers, where their price now shot up from two for five cents to as high as twenty cents. Particularly in demand was the two-volume biography of Hook by R. H. Dalton Barham, published in 1849, and the shorter memoir written by John G. Lockhart, Sir Walter Scott's son-in-law, published in 1853. Each contained an admiring account of Hook's irrepressible wit, a description of many of his practical jokes including the Berners Street hoax and an appraisal of his astonishing literary and carousing career. The most intense study, however, bore on the niceties of his jokesmanship, particularly in his acknowledged masterwork on Berners Street.

The chief argument of the many who placed Hook second to the unknown American was that the latter's conception had been grander and that his technique—except for a slight uncertainty in the Boden sequence and a failure to bring it to its full possibilities—was everywhere able to achieve it. A theme so ambitious could easily have fallen down in execution. Instead of limiting himself to one victim, Gentleman Joe had introduced several sub-victims, at first entirely unconnected, and had slowly, gradually, and with the priceless element of surprise, woven them together in his design. One had to admire the contrapuntal skill with which the Dix, Buckley, Boden, Irish famine and mayor of Paterson themes, so soft and remote at first, were drawn together fortissimo. For all his craft, Hook had not caused a victim to be accused of theft and murder within two hours, an achievement many observers ranked as one of the best in Joe's repertoire. His use of the New York *Herald* in luring a few more sub-victims into the scheme added pleasing grace-notes, and no one could underestimate his facility or his background of churchly knowledge in his hoodwinking of the clergy. The most important of Joe's letters were published in the papers, drawing praise for their style and urbanity, which made some readers facetiously compare him with Addison or Congreve. Others of a bookish turn swore that Joe was the real-life reincarnation of the seventeenth-century Spanish *picaro*, a rogue with so much wit and dash that one could forgive him for actions that were, strictly interpreted, reprehensible.

The question that excited literally hundreds of thousands of readers in the metropolitan area extending well beyond Paterson was, who was Joe? As always with such mysteries, a few wiseacres pretending to inside knowledge started unreliable rumors: Joe was a jealous assistant minister at Trinity; he was George Francis Train, the millionaire crank who liked to poke fun at the social establishment; he was a prankish student at the General Theological Seminary; he was a *Herald* feature writer.

This last theory gained some support because Joe's letters and activities constantly publicized the *Herald*, its classified department and its Irish-relief campaign, a huge enterprise that was preparing to send the *S. S. Constellation* to Ireland with $300,000 worth of provisions and clothing. All the other newspapers covering the case were forced to name the *Herald* repeatedly, a necessity that galled them, for it was already the richest paper in the country. Its shrewd, convivial owner, Bennett—the man who had sent Stanley to find Livingstone in the first place—was famous for his eccentricities, drunk or sober. No one had forgotten the paper's sensational scoop six years earlier. The front page of its issue on the morning of November 9, 1874, had been devoted to sanguinary reports on the accidental escape of all the wild animals in the Central Park zoo. Under headlines such as "Terrible Scenes of Mutilation" and "A Shocking Sabbath Carnival of Death," the *Herald* had told of elephants and lions rampaging the city streets, killing forty-nine and injuring or trampling two hundred, and of sturdy old Governor Dix himself stalking out and shooting a Bengal tiger. New York was in a panic. Citizens barred their doors, got out muskets and prayed for the safe return of relatives, very few having read the notice in small type at the bottom of the page that the story was a fabrication intended to "test the city's preparedness to meet a catastrophe." If Bennett could do that, it was not implausible to picture him assigning one of his cleverest writers to send out all those letters, then sitting back in glee to listen to his competitors' teeth grind as they were compelled to puff the *Herald* or miss the year's most unusual story.

While the newspapers tried to keep a straight face in their front-page summations of the case, there were times when something like levity broke through. The coverage was what the quiet rector would have called sensational. Most New Yorkers rejected the idea that Joe might be dangerous. Such a master of whimsy, it was felt, would not harm a fly. Colonel Bliss, a man of gravity and propriety, told reporters sourly that he failed to see anything sidesplitting in the machinations of a blackmailer who could well be desperate and vicious, nor about Theodore Hook either.

"Dr. Dix says he is not aware of any person who would be actuated by feelings of revenge to do this," Bliss said. "Still, Dr. Dix may have an enemy and not know it. Gentlemen at the head of large corporations are often held responsible for things of which they are quite ignorant."

Here was a persuasive theory. Trinity Parish had enemies galore, even among other Episcopalians. To settle a score against the parish by hounding the rector was a device of which some mentalities were quite capable. The parish's property holdings, mistakenly believed to be worth $60,000,000 or more, had aroused jealousy for decades. The jealousy was augmented by the fact that among the church's communicants were Astors, De Lanceys, Ciscos, Jays and other wealthy families who, it was felt, hardly needed such capitalization. Along with its original land grant from the English crown, Trinity had been given title to all "drift whales" found in the harbor or on the nearby coast. It had never exercised this right, but there were those who accused it of grabbing everything else in sight and of being unscrupulous in its control of its secular property.

The hatred had begun at the time of the Revolution, when Trinity had remained loyal to the crown longer than was expedient. The New York State Assembly, irate that this nest of Tories should retain the profits of its affection for the king, tried but failed to enact a law stripping the parish of the revenue from its property. In 1857, other New York Episcopal churches, claiming that Trinity had never held sole title to the property, introduced a bill in the legislature that would have wrested it away and given its control to the whole diocese. The measure was narrowly defeated, thanks to General John Dix's convincing arguments against it and to State Senator Daniel E. Sickles' able support of Trinity, but the bitterness still lingered.

There was a widespread feeling that the parish was selfishly hoarding a treasure it had acquired through merest chance.

Trinity, on the contrary, could point to outright grants it had given to needy churches and colleges (not always Episcopalian) in New York State and elsewhere totaling some $2,500,000 since the Revolution. It had given money or land to scores of institutions such as King's College (Columbia College after the Revolution), St. Mark's Church, Grace Church, the Society for the Promotion of Religion and Learning and Hobart College. It was regarded as an eleemosynary foundation and it received constant appeals for help. When General Dix became a vestryman he was alarmed at the size of these expenditures. He had recommended a tightening of the purse strings, arguing that the patrimony should not be scattered abroad but should be held in trust for the gospelizing of the poor in the church's Lower Manhattan parish. As a result, the pleas of other churches for financial aid were more often rejected, causing ill-feeling.

Indeed, for almost one hundred and forty years there had been incessant claims that Trinity did not even own its property and was holding it illegally. Some sixty-three acres of its original land grant had earlier been included in a farm owned by the Dutch widow Anneke Jans Bogardus, extending from what later became Broadway to the Hudson, its southern boundary roughly at the present Warren Street, its northern at Watts Street. Vrouw Bogardus died in 1663. In 1664 the British forced the Dutch to capitulate and New Amsterdam became New York. In 1670 the land was sold in behalf of Vrouw Bogardus' eight children to Francis Lovelace, the English governor of the colony. But soon it was confiscated by the Duke of York because "Lovelace was as deeply in debt to him as to every one else." In 1705 the "Bogardus" land, along with two other large parcels which had never belonged to the Bogardus family, was granted by Queen Anne to Trinity Parish, which had been chartered by William III in 1697. These combined holdings—still farm and pasture—stretched from the present Fulton Street on the south to Christopher Street on the north.

However, the 1670 sale of the Bogardus land to Lovelace had not been executed by Cornelius, one of the Widow Bogardus' children—an omission that could be construed as invalidating the contract. Starting in 1746, people claiming to be descendants of Cornelius Bogardus had repeatedly sued Trinity not only for recovery of the property but for an accounting of incomes the church had received. But if there were contractual lapses clouding Trinity's original title, the statute of limitations had nullified them. The parish's title had been firmly upheld. Since that time Trinity had answered suits simply by relying on its established title rather than answering specific charges of claimants. This strategy was often interpreted as an admission that fraud was involved and that the parish was "hiding" behind the statute of limitations. As the city expanded northward and Trinity's glebe became the very heart of the metropolis, it was subdivided by the Trinity corporation into more than 2,000 lots of enormous value which constantly grew even more valuable. This island of riches was eyed covetously from all sides. The claimants increased in number with its increase in value. An 1847 "Bogardus" suit against Trinity was thrown out on the usual grounds, the judge adding that after the passing of five generations "the descendants of Anneke Jans, at this day, are hundreds, if not thousands, in number."

The persistence of these hopeless efforts became a perennial joke in the city's legal establishment. The plaintiffs invariably placed fantastic value on lands that were precious enough in reality. One happy batch of Bogardus claimants estimated that the money due them with interest was "from $500,000,000 to $750,000,000, of which $80,000,000 is in actual cash held by the Bank of Holland." Some of the suits even demanded the return of Trinity lands that had never been part of the Bogardus farm. In some instances, honest people who believed themselves or actually were Bogardus descendants fell into the hands of shyster lawyers who accepted fat fees even though they knew the title was unassailable. No sooner was one drove of Bogarduses disillusioned than a bigger one sprang up elsewhere. Bogarduses appeared from New Jersey, Pennsylvania, Ohio, Michigan, Illinois, California and, of all places, Halifax, Nova Scotia. In 1867 an association of heirs from various parts of the country was formed at the Astor House in New York, calling itself the Anneke Jans Association and vowing to force Trinity to disgorge its illegal wealth. Although they lost like all the rest, the newspapers commented from time to time on the great value of the land and the various Bogardus lawsuits—publicity which never failed to turn up new Bogardus claimants.

For example, an 1873 New York *World* account of the by then more than century-old succession of Bogardus claims inspired one Emma H. Wallace of Chicago. Saying that she could prove herself in the direct bloodline (always the essential first step in these cases), she came to New York, organized a joint stock company and held meetings in Manhattan and Brooklyn to raise money to fight her case. She sold shares at ten dollars and five dollars, promising proportionate payments out of the millions that would be hers when justice was done. Her case against Trinity was ultimately dismissed, but not before lawyers had used up the money and made her stock valueless.

Even now, at the time that Gentleman Joe's postcards were falling like hailstones, a man named Van Giesen (who of course claimed direct descent) saw the difficulties of challenging Trinity through the usual legal avenues and tried another. Declaring that the records did not show that the Anneke Jans Bogardus estate had ever been administered and settled, he applied to the surrogate for letters of administration. He would ultimately be denied by the state's highest court. The Bogardus claims had come to be a sour joke to Dr. Dix and the vestrymen. They found it necessary to have a form letter printed to answer inquiries from Bogardus heirs who continued to write in (or more often to have their attorneys write in) to say that they had just discovered that Trinity had appropriated their property and had better return it fast.

All this convinced Colonel Bliss that Gentleman Joe might be found among (a) Episcopalians or others angered because Trinity had rejected their pleas for money grants, or (b) resentful Bogardus claimants. This scarcely narrowed the field, since there had been many rejections and there were many Bogarduses. Still, Dr. Dix and other church functionaries were urged to search their memories for outstanding soreheads, and the parish's mail was combed again. The suspicions within Trinity Church were by no means eliminated, however, and feeling among its personnel was reaching a critical point. As a portentous *Times* editorial put it:

> So long as he [Joe] remained undetected, the gossips suspected High Church and Low Church functionaries, laymen, jealous neighbors, disappointed candidates for canonical honors, and each other. Nobody can ever know how far the foundations of society have been undermined by the unjust suspicions which the mystery of the anonymous letters... has engendered.

The hope that the enormous newspaper publicity given the case might bring in information leading to the guilty man's arrest dwindled day by day. But it was taken for granted that this publicity meant the end of Joe's harassments, for two reasons: surely he was too frightened by it to continue his work; and even if he was not, the whole city now knew of the victimization of Dr. Dix and Buckley and would, of course, not be misled by any further bogus postcards. The many citizens who had become enthusiasts in Hookiana and connoisseurs of jokesmanship faced the grim prospect of gnawing their nails in perpetual frustration if Joe should choose to fade out of sight forever, although this very thing was the dearest wish of Dr. Dix.

CHAPTER VIII

THE CIRCUS WILL BEGIN AT 8½

Joe, however, had unlimited daring and resourcefulness as well as a mastery of the dramatic pause rivaling that of Mark Twain, who was then mesmerizing smaller audiences from the lecture platform. On St. Patrick's Day, March seventeenth, while New York's Irish staged an "austerity" parade in order to send more money to the homeland, Joe's campaign entered its second phase. After a three-week lull, Dr. Dix received a letter in the same old hand. It promised that the siege of the rector's house would resume on Friday, March nineteenth, unless he met a slightly altered stipulation.

"You can avoid this, as you can all future annoyances," it read, "by paying over to me $1,500. I have concluded to raise my price $500." The writer, dropping his pretext that he was an old classmate trying to shield Dr. Dix from another's machinations, instructed him to "answer through personals to Reddy, in Herald Friday. I will enter to your lecture to-night with pleasure, also your sermon next Sunday at old Trinity. Yours in the Lord."

The signature was entirely illegible, which really made no differ-ence. At the same time the editor of the *Times* received a letter from the apostle of anarchy, reading:

My Dear Sir: Sickness has prevented me from writing before to thank you for your charming and delightful two-column article which appeared in your valuable journal of the 13th inst. in regard to myself and my distinguished friend, the Rev. Morgan Dix, S. T. D., Rector of Trinity Church, New-York. It seldom happens that so much pleasure is given so cheaply.... I wish to correct two or three little inaccuracies which appeared. In the first place I did not invite thousands of people to my dear Rector's house. I only asked in all Five Hundred. Secondly, Dr. Dix is mistaken if he thinks he has no enemies, although person-ally I am very fond of him, to prove which I will be at his lecture this evening at Trinity Chapel, and next Sunday morning I will occupy my usual seat at old Trinity—dear old Trinity... and will call again with the hosts of others who will honor him on Friday next. Please be pres-ent and witness the event. He knows how to stop the trouble, but not through the infernal newspapers... believe me, dear Mr. Editor, yours very respectfully,

—High Churchman

The thought that the humorist regularly sat in a Trinity pew—might even be a well-known and devout communicant—added fur-ther interest to the mystery. The *Tribune* also received a note from High Churchman, who seemed not to miss a line published in any of the papers:

Dear Sir: Permit me to thank you very sincerely for your delightful and entertaining account of the trouble between Rev. Morgan Dix and myself but there were several little inaccuracies. I only sent 500 postal cards, but have issued several hundred for to-morrow (Friday). The

circus will begin at 8½ and last all day. I will be on hand. I don't know
any Mr. Buckley, but possibly some of my friends do....

Dr. Dix was still firm in his determination not to deal with his
tormentor. Colonel Bliss, however, refused to let slip any opportunity to establish contact with Gentleman Joe-High Churchman-
Reddy and possibly lead him into a rendezvous at which he might be
trapped. Unknown to the rector, Bliss inserted a personal in Friday
morning's *Herald*, reading:

REDDY—If good faith is secured something can be done.

Among the followers of Gentleman Joe there was frank disappointment. One of his most endearing qualities had been his intelligence, which now seemed in eclipse. He should know that the
publicity given the persecution of Dr. Dix would prevent anyone
but outright simpletons from falling for the same hoax. The rector
agreed. He had an early breakfast and went to his downtown office
overlooking St. Paul's churchyard, not because he feared any throng
of visitors but because this was his Friday routine.

Nevertheless, about a hundred people gathered outside the rectory that snowy morning. Some were newspaper readers anxious to
see with their own eyes what tomfoolery might take place. At least
two dozen were reporters, under orders not to miss even the slightest
nuance of this continuing drama. Also present were Captain Byrnes,
Colonel Bliss and four detectives. It was not forgotten that Joe had
promised to be there himself, and although no one had any idea of
his appearance, the four were ready to collar him if he should some-
how betray himself.

Astonishingly, there was enough activity to cause the *Tribune*
to headline next morning, FIFTY CALLS ON DR. DIX. A Post Office
employee clad like a servant answered the door. The calls began

promptly at 8:30, as Joe had promised, and were well spaced throughout the day. The preponderance of visitors were unemployed footmen, waiters, housemaids, coachmen and a few wetnurses, all of whom had advertised in the *Herald* for work. But there was also a sprinkling of merchants seeking business. Among them were several undertakers ready to supervise obsequies, one tattoo specialist who came prepared to emblazon a spread eagle in three colors on the chest of the gentleman of the house, and four lawyers eager to advise Mrs. Dix on how to institute divorce proceedings. This large turnout in the face of publicity that should have precluded it was due to Gentleman Joe's cunning in sending his dupes simply to the address without mentioning the Dix name. The lawyers, for example, one of them described as "a member of a firm in high standing and widely known," had received the following message enclosed in an envelope:

> Dear Sir: I am about to bring an action for divorce. Of course, I do not wish to go to your office, and would like to have you call and see me at my house, No. 27 West Twenty-fifth-street. Ask for Mrs. D. Come about 5½ o'clock and oblige.
>
> —Mrs. D.

Among other callers were a representative of the New York, Havana and Mexican Mail Line bringing two tickets for Havana; and a man from the Cunard Line with two tickets for Liverpool. Another gentleman, who had lost two $1,000 bonds through what he was certain was theft, had advertised in the *Herald* for them, offering $100 reward. He had received a postcard telling him he could pick up the bonds at 27 West Twenty-fifth Street by paying the reward. He brought a private detective along with him and prearranged a signal: if he went inside and got the bonds, he would scratch his leg on leaving, whereupon the eye, watching from a doorway opposite, would dash into the house and arrest the thief. As the *World* put it, "The gentleman was scratching his head instead of his leg as he emerged."

Thus the lone, indomitable man of letters had vindicated himself, proven wrong those of his admirers who had lost faith in him and won another round against the massed forces of law and order. If Joe was among the spectators on Twenty-fifth Street, he went undetected. The same was true of Dr. Dix's Lenten lecture at Trinity Chapel and the Sunday-morning service at old Trinity, both of which Joe had promised to attend. Among those in the pews at these meetings were several fairly hard-eyed men whose tailoring was not equal to that of the average parishioner. They were Byrnes' detectives. They were looking for a man who could only give himself away by some exotic behavior. They did not find him.

Closer students of Theodore Hook saw in this another refinement which Gentleman Joe had borrowed from the Englishman but had signally improved. Both masters had taken pride in their work and had gone to some pains to see it in operation—Hook from a point across the street. But Joe's superiority lay in his ability to prolong and diversify his operations so that ultimately, through his own letters (most of them published in the newspapers), he was in actual communication with the police, commenting on their work and telling them where he might be found. This was a conception so original as to come near meriting the adjective "inspired." It was often jeeringly said that the police could not catch a suspect even if they had his name, address, description, photograph and one hand on his shoulder. The spectacle of the detectives searching conscientiously for someone they would not recognize if they saw him was a diverting one, particularly if Joe was there taking it in.

CHAPTER IX

TRINITY'S GIN MILLS AND BROTHELS

New Yorkers who had missed Joe during his three-week vacation from delinquency welcomed him back to the headlines. The city's newspapermen were again seized by polarity. The papers could not conceal their editors' fondness for the misdoer who relieved the March doldrums and brightened all their lives. Yet in their editorials they fulfilled the convention that illegality must be denounced—a case of Page Four demanding the arrest of the man whom Page One held in greatest affection and hoped would continue his work indefinitely. A *Times* editorial said in part:

> It seems obvious that the ingenious persecutor of the Rev. Dr. Dix is quite as much bent on gratifying a morbid desire for notoriety as for satisfying personal malice or extorting black-mail.... It will be the reverse of creditable to our detective force if they should be foiled by a person who takes so little pains to cover up his tracks as the persecutor of the Rector of Trinity.

Little pains! This was a libel against a man who seemed to take exceptional pains. The vigil at the Fifth Avenue mailboxes had been resumed, but here again the watchers were foiled, for Joe's next letter was mailed not on Fifth Avenue but at a station near Eighth Avenue and Thirty-fourth Street. It was a very hasty note received by the *Tribune* indicating that Joe felt remorse over sending unemployed domestic servants to the Dix house only to meet with disappointment—suggesting also that he was either smelling of the cork or was out of his mind:

> Dr. Sir   I am sorry I played that game—it will not occur again— very Respectfully yours
>
> (I can't help it to-day—it is too late, but it will not occur next week—please destroy this)

There was no signature but the hand was unmistakable. The envelope bore the imprint of the Fifth Avenue Hotel, while the message itself was scribbled on a yellow Western Union telegraph blank, folded and addressed on the back "To the Rev. Morgan Dix, D.D.," as if Joe had first planned to send it directly to Dix. A detail of detectives pounded into the swank Fifth Avenue, which faced Madison Square and was just around the corner from the rectory. It seemed quite likely that Joe had been among the crowd watching the goings-on at the rectory that day and had stopped in at the hotel after enjoying his handiwork.

But the Fifth Avenue was a big hostelry and no one there remembered a man who could not be described at all except that he might have spent a minute or two at a desk in the lobby, writing a note on a telegraph blank.

Although the investigators already had more categories of potential suspects than they could easily handle, Joe's latest cognomen of High Churchman supplied a whole new congregation. At Trinity,

Morgan Dix had become involved in the quarrel between High and Low Church interpretations of Episcopal doctrine that aroused unholy bitterness. While a student at the theological seminary, he had been enkindled by the Oxford Movement spreading to this country from England, which aimed to restore the ancient Catholic liturgy to divine services. When the English threw out the Pope, they had chucked most of his accouterments with him. The Oxford faction felt that this had stripped the ceremony of hallowed ritual and left it as perfunctory as retail trade. These reformers insisted that they did not want to restore the Pope but only his liturgy. Their followers had gradually resumed the use of ceremonial vestments and beliefs such as the acceptance of transubstantiation, which to the puritanical Evangelicals or Low Church faction smacked of "romanism and popery." The strife had split Episcopalians in twain. The secession of some of the Oxford reformers, including the famous John Henry Newman, to the Roman Catholic Church had convinced many Lows that High Church Episcopalianism was actually a stepping stone back to Romanism—a suspicion augmented as recently as 1879 when Pope Leo XII had created Newman a cardinal.

Dr. Dix was the most prominent champion of the High Church movement in America—"so high," it was said, "that he would sit atop the steeple if he could." He believed firmly in ceremony, which he considered divinely inspired, lending dignity and beauty to the services. At Trinity's seven churches his priests were clad in traditional robes, the choirs were vested in cottas, the altars were decorated with flowers and candles, and daily celebrations of the Eucharist were held. He had given his hearty support to the founding of the Sisterhood of St. Mary and became chaplain of this first full-fledged Episcopal religious order in this country. The Evangelicals had erupted over what they termed sure evidence of popery—nuns under perpetual vows and led by a Mother Superior.

Not surprisingly, the rector was regarded by some Evangelicals as the head and front of an infamous plot to betray the Episcopal Church and lead it back to Rome. It was felt that he was using Trinity's millions in doctrinal bribery to bring this about. As one church-oriented publication, the *Independent Statesman*, put it:

> Trinity Church wields an immense influence through the entire State of New York by lending money for building Churches; it advances from $1500 to $5000 on mortgage, with the tacit understanding that ritualism is to be favored; so long as this is done the payment of interest is waived; and in this manner the Churches in the interior of the State have been brought over to the High Church Party.

Dr. Dix rebutted the charge with his unfailing dignity. Ritualism, he said, was never a factor in Trinity's loans or grants, which had gone to several Low churches, among them St. George's on Stuyvesant Square, "of which the venerable, estimable and honored Dr. [Stephen H.] Tyng, my kind personal friend, is Rector."

But was it not possible that Joe, who now called himself High Churchman, was actually a Low Churchman taking revenge?

Ritualism aside, there were those who felt that General Dix and his son Morgan had long constituted a sort of dictatorship over Trinity's real-estate holdings and administered it in a high-handed manner. Jealous critics pointed out how dumb-lucky the parish was to be so rich in the first place. As this line of reasoning went, Trinity was lucky in getting an early start in New York, lucky that the British happened to drive out the Dutch, lucky that its denomination happened to be the state church of England, lucky that Governor Lovelace lost the Bogardus farm to the Duke of York through debt, lucky that Queen Anne had indulged a whim of generosity toward the parish, lucky that New York City had grown so fantastically and lucky that American law had not upset the grant of a rejected sovereign. The Revolution had beaten the redcoats and disowned the king, and yet Trinity remained the most affluent vestige of British imperialism left in America.

On top of this, the Panic of 1873, misleadingly named since some of its worst effects were felt five years later, had caused one hundred and fifty tenants of Trinity to organize early in 1878 in an effort to get a reduction in their leases. Admitting that "for nearly 150 years Trinity Church was proverbial for its liberality to its tenants," they felt that liberality had given way to hard business practice. Most of these tenants were landlords themselves, owning houses or office buildings on land leased from the church. They declared that because of the general business depression they could not get enough in rents to meet their own lease costs. They sent a committee headed by George M. Chapman to call on General Dix, asking that ground rentals be reduced 25 to 35 per cent when their leases expired in May.

While both Dixes were powerful at Trinity, they ruled at least theoretically at the pleasure of the vestry, and the general's policies as comptroller were dictated by that body. The vestry had followed a policy of fair dealing toward tenants that did not extend to charity (and it had to be admitted that there were some Trinity-owned tenements that did not reflect credit on the church). The property was a gift of God that had to be husbanded in God's service. As General Dix told the committee, "The corporation is desirous of treating its tenants fairly, and at the same time to keep its own interests in view." But he pointed out that Trinity had not raised the price of its leases when times had been good and that a 25 per cent reduction was impossible. A 10 per cent drop might be considered. Although there was some grumbling, the tenants and the church had come to terms.

News stories about the matter had interested the editors of the Boston *Index*, a free-thinkers' publication. These godless people, after doing some quick and inexact research, published a long article headed, ASTOUNDING FACTS ABOUT TRINITY CHURCH, declaring that Trinity owned 5,000 city lots "worth fully seventy millions of dollars" and paid no taxes on them. Then the *Index* unloaded a haymaker:

> According to the official records of the offices of the Chief of Police and the Excise Commissioners, the real estate of Trinity Church supports SEVEN HUNDRED AND SIXTY-FOUR LIQUOR SALOONS or gin-mills, and NINETY-SIX KNOWN HOUSES OF PROSTITUTION (ninety-two white and four colored), with many others suspected to be such.

This sounded so much like a description of the nether reaches of the Tenderloin rather than church-owned property that the story was picked up by the lay press in Boston and elsewhere. The sensation it created could hardly have been exceeded by news revelations of the discovery that Queen Victoria had taken a lover. The Trinity vestry went into hurried session and General Dix was authorized to lay these scurrilous charges. Since the parish's original good luck, succeeding vestries had taken the lordly attitude that it was no one's business how much property Trinity owned or what was done with it—a policy continued under the Dixes. This corporate secrecy had had the effect of causing exaggerated estimates of the property and impairing public good will—or, more accurately, increasing public disfavor.

The general was forced to open the moneybags a trifle and permit some rubbernecking in order to rout the enemy. He composed a long letter which he sent not only to the *Index* but to *The Churchman* and to the Boston and New York daily newspapers. Trinity, he said, now owned only seven hundred and fifty lots valued at hardly more than one-tenth of what the *Index* claimed, and "we pay taxes on every foot of ground used for secular purposes," the only property escaping taxes being the actual church edifices, schoolhouses and cemeteries. Slightly more than $100,000 in taxes had been paid that year, plus assessments. Of the saloon and prostitution charges he wrote:

> The utter recklessness of this accusation cannot be better illustrated than by the statement of the fact that the alleged number of liquor-saloons and houses of prostitution is 860, exceeding by 110 the whole number of lots owned by Trinity Church. If the accusation were true, there would be a liquor-saloon on every lot belonging to this corporation, and on 96 of its lots a liquor-saloon and a house of prostitution. The charge is destitute even of a shadow of foundation. The number of lots of which the corporation has the entire control is 483. On 259 of these the lessees own the houses. On 224 the houses belong to the Church.... On all the leases of these 483 lots there has been for years a covenant on the part of the lessees that no intoxicating liquors shall be sold on the premises.
>
> ...I say, without fear of contradiction, that there is not a single liquor-saloon or "gin-mill" on any of these 483 lots. It is proper to add that there are 267 lots held for long terms on old leases. Over these the corporation has no control but a ground rent is regularly collected, and the vestry have no knowledge, nor do the records of the Police or Excise Departments show, that any one of them is used for either of the purposes alleged by your informant.

Here General Dix produced letters from the chief of police and the head of the Excise Department attesting that there were no known gin mills or brothels on any of the property. To the *Index* he finished:

> I might well be pardoned the strongest expression of indignation at these calumnious accusations against Trinity Church, but I withhold it from the belief that you have published them without any suspicion

of their untruth and that you will cheerfully give the same publicity to their refutation.

Indeed, for Dr. Dix to say that he had no enemies was to say that there were no leaves in Vallombrosa and no sand in Sahara. To them could be added the nation's feminists, who hated him with passion and unanimity. True, Gentleman Joe's handwriting was unquestionably that of a man, but it was also true that the feminists had some strong masculine support.

In 1880 the women fighting for some improvement in their voteless, voiceless, second-class existence found Morgan Dix battling them every step of the way. He insisted that woman's place was not only in the home but in the background. He had been appalled by the progress of such advocates as Elizabeth Cady Stanton and Susan B. Anthony. The firmest of fundamentalists, he could quote the Bible endlessly in support of his belief that it was sinful not only for women to complain of their lot but to make public speeches or to engage in any activities normally reserved for men, or to modify their dangerously long skirts and to wear clothing in any degree similar to those of men, such as the accursed baggy pantaloons made famous by Amelia Bloomer.

"That a woman should dress as a man, and talk like a man, and act like a man, was abomination in the sight of Jehovah," he said in one of his sermons, and went on to quote St. Paul: "'I suffer not a woman to teach, nor to usurp authority over the man, but to be in silence. For Adam was first formed, then Eve.'"

The feminist appeal for "higher education" for women, he insisted, was one aspect of their subversion. The founding in recent years of Vassar, Smith and Wellesley as institutions on the collegiate level for women had shaken him. Many of their graduates refused to be in silence. In fact, some were going on to usurp man's place as doctors, lawyers, professors and even ministers. What aroused him

more was the decision of a few great state universities in the West
to follow the lead of Oberlin College in permitting young men and
women to *attend the same classes.*

"Some of the advocates of higher education," he said in one lecture, "...demand what is known by the term—which I ask your pardon for using here—co-education. By co-education is meant, not
only that the youth of both sexes should be taught the very same
things, but that they should be taught in the same places, and out
of the same books, and by the same teachers, and in the company of
each other." This made the debasing of innocent girls inevitable. "A
friend of mine saw, at Zurich in Switzerland, young women walking
about in trousers, smoking cigarettes, and chatting with their professors; they were medical students. An eye-witness told me that he
saw young girls parading on the campus of a Western college with
the sophomoric 'banger' [cane] grasped in the hand." He quoted
with distaste part of a letter received from a young man who had
recently transferred from the Episcopal Racine College: "The school
I go to now is a dandy one. Girls go to this school as well as boys;
and we have a bully time at a party every Friday evening, playing
kissing games with 'em."

At this very moment, as a trustee and a power at Columbia College, he was fighting Columbia's President F. A. P. Barnard's campaign to establish collegiate education for women and was stunned
to learn that two Columbia professors were already allowing a few
women to attend men's classes informally. He saw the moral retro-
gression of the female as an international phenomenon, instigated
by false leaders, some of them clearly in the hands of the devil.
While he agreed that George Eliot's *Middlemarch* was "fascinating,
brilliant, powerful," he also found it "cruel and cold as the devil
and death" because of its protagonist Dorothea's discovery that
the male-dominated society refused to give other than trivial and
demeaning chores to women qualified for work demanding the

highest intelligence and ability. Dr. Dix, not forgetting the novelist's unhallowed union with G. H. Lewes, incontinently called her a
"malevolent romancer." He said, "Now this is one-sided and unreal
from first to last... there is work to do." But when it came down to
specifics it was the home he was thinking of: "Shame on the woman
who calls any education *higher* than that which qualifies her for her
place as regent in such a domain!" The campaign by feminists for
more liberal divorce laws, he felt, was part and parcel of a diaboli-
cal effort to break up the home. Divorce was already too easy rather
than too hard: "When things reach the state toward which we have
been drifting... we shall have reached the condition of the Mormon,
with this sole difference, that his polygamy is simultaneous and
ours consecutive."

If he feared Mrs. Stanton and Miss Anthony, he was utterly
revolted by their former friend, Victoria Woodhull, who for ten
years had been streaking across the New York firmament like a
sinuous comet. There were rumors that she and her equally bizarre
sister, Tennie C. Claflin, had bewitched Commodore Vanderbilt into
setting them up in the brokerage business on Wall Street, where
they prospered. The sisters gave public speeches. They were spiri-
tualists and trance-physicians as well as feminists. Mrs. Woodhull
had divorced her first husband, a dipsomaniac and drug addict, but
permitted him to live in her household with her second husband,
whom she also ultimately divorced. She announced herself a candidate for President on the Cosmo-Political party ticket. It was she, in
her personal newspaper, *Woodhull & Claflin's Weekly*, who had made
the public charges of adultery against Henry Ward Beecher which
ultimately erupted in the inconclusive but ruinous one-hundred-
and-twelve-day trial of Beecher. She had been jailed briefly for mailing "obscenities." For months she had been the mistress of Theodore
Tilton. In a Steinway Hall lecture she had shouted, "Yes, I am a free
lover! I have an inalienable, constitutional and natural right to love

whom I may, to love as long or short a period as I can, to change that love every day if I please!"

Although Mrs. Stanton and Miss Anthony had cooled toward her, Victoria Woodhull had succeeded in linking the whole feminist movement—already known for its impiety—with sexual license and other forms of depravity. To Dr. Dix it seemed certain that if one explored under her rather pretty head of hair one would find horns. He attacked many aspects of feminism and was attacked by feminists in return.

Perhaps it was no more absurd to think it possible that some follower of the feminists might be punishing him by adroit misuse of the mails than to believe that such a creature as Victoria Woodhull existed, as she indubitably did. But surely the greatest absurdity of all was to place any hope in the "Find the enemy, find the criminal" theory. The rector of Trinity had enemies in the hundreds and thousands. They might be found among feminists, suffragists, atheists, Low Church fanatics, Bogardus claimants, disgruntled employees of Trinity Church or its chapels or its corporation, rejected applicants for a loan or grant, or angry tenants. To these enemies, in fact, could be added a good many thousand more who might be called bell-tax protesters. The bells in Trinity's steeple, far and away the best in town, traditionally played by official request on secular festal days such as Washington's Birthday. For this Trinity charged the city a fee for the pay of the bell-ringer and the wear on the bells—a custom that continuously drew angry complaints from many citizens.

Logic, usually so helpful in crime detection through its narrowing of the field, here widened it with every new effort of the brain. It was hardly surprising that Colonel Bliss was in a dilemma, or that Captain Byrnes' detectives and Superintendent Gayler's Post Office men were running around in circles in their efforts to find enemies of Dr. Dix. The records showed clearly that there were enemies behind every lamp post and mailbox—indeed, in many a pew.

CHAPTER X

HOT ON THE TRAIL

If some shameless citizens loved Gentleman Joe, the investigators had come to detest him. A few news stories were so worded as to satirize their efforts, and a few editorials showed impatience with them for their failure to solve the mystery. To this was added Joe's obvious enjoyment of the newspaper attention he had won, his habit of playing up to the press and his latest and most cheeky device of all—notifying the papers in advance of his next foray and carrying it off successfully despite all the lawmen's strenuous efforts. By now the latter were convinced that it was Joe's deliberate intention to make them look silly. In their humiliation they were panting to catch him. They argued hotly among themselves as to whether his intentions were felonious or only jocular, but they were in perfect agreement that he must be found quickly or they would lose whatever shreds of reputation remained to them.

Ominously, the relations between the city detective force and Gayler's men were less than cordial. The detectives regarded the Post

Office crowd as amateurs who had better stick to cancelling stamps, while the latter felt that Byrnes' sleuths were no more than ignorant flatfeet who would still be pounding beats but for political preferment. The Post Office Inspection Service easily had the advantage of age, having been chasing mail robbers for a century. Being a secret service, small in numbers, it was little known and it was not until 1872 and 1873 that Congress expanded its duties by passing laws forbidding the mailing of material that was fraudulent, threatening, obscene or otherwise illegal. The smut-obsessed Anthony Comstock had thereupon become New York's most active postal inspector. But since he was interested only in obscenity, which kept him busy night and day, he disregarded the matter of Gentleman Joe. Though Gayler had risen above his former job of postal inspector, he was so well liked by Colonel Bliss and Dr. Dix that he had been placed in charge of the Post Office Department's probe.

At this point the two investigative bodies, pledged to work in sweet comity and cooperation, began to draw apart. A close reading of contemporary accounts suggests that Bliss and Dix contributed to the jealousy between the two forces by favoring the Post Office men. This would be natural for the rector, since his father had once been postmaster in the city and Gayler, a man of quiet conscientiousness, had worked under him. The rector's hatred of sensationalism also militated against Byrnes and his crew, who constantly appeared in lurid newspaper accounts of crime. Perhaps two other factors were the belief that city detectives were low ruffians hardly better than the criminals they hunted, and the impression made by Captain Byrnes himself. The captain was a fine figure of a man until he opened his mouth, when he did shocking violence to grammar and pronunciation—a failing that would grate on cultivated men like Dix and Bliss.

As for Byrnes himself, he was in pain for he had a considerable reputation to lose. A man of prodigious memory, he carried a card-file of criminals in his brain and was an adroit questioner who could often trip a suspect into a confession without the usual persuasion of the time—beatings with a rubber hose. He was one of those legendary detectives whom the public credited with an almost magic skill. The magic, he knew, was dwindling fast, and if anyone wanted to see Joe behind bars it was Thomas Byrnes. Furthermore, Dr. Dix had influential friends who were not afraid to apply pressure at the very top. Mayor Cooper was telling District Attorney Phelps that Joe must be caught, and Phelps was pressing Police Chief Walling, who was importuning Byrnes, who was prodding his detectives. Postmaster General David Key sent word to Postmaster James of the importance of capturing the desecrator of the mails—a warning James passed on to Gayler, and Gayler to his men.

Colonel Bliss had set great store by his theory that Gentleman Joe was indeed an extortionist and would establish contact by replying to Bliss's personal in the *Herald* addressed to Reddy. That hope was blasted. Joe did not reply. Daniel Buckley, however, received a chaste note signed in Dr. Dix's name and reading, "My dear Mr. Buckley, if you will be so kind as to call at my home to-morrow at five for whiskey, we can discuss matters of mutual interest. May God guide your steps!" Buckley looked hard at it. Again there had been an attempt to disguise the hand, but he recognized the flowing script nevertheless.

On Saturday, March twentieth, there were no mistaken callers at the rectory. Buckley was also free from trouble, and there was no word that Joe had fixed on a new victim. That afternoon, Captain Byrnes had a visit from Samuel T. Peters of the brokerage firm of Williams & Peters in the Cotton Exchange. Peters had just returned from a business trip to New Orleans and had read the newspaper accounts of the persecution of Dr. Dix for the first time. They had given him quite a start, because seven years earlier he had encountered a case so similar that he felt there must be a connection.

In 1873, he related, when he was in London on business he had stayed at the Langham Hotel in Mayfair, always a rendezvous for visiting Americans. There he had met another guest, E. Fairfax Williamson, whom he had known very slightly in New York. Williamson, always the very glass of fashion, surprised Peters by the warmth of his greeting, shaking his hand and expressing pleasure as if they were very old and dear friends. His eagerness took on meaning when he confided that he was in a scrape and would be delighted if Peters would go to court and vouch for his character. It turned out that Williamson, after quarreling with his former friend and landlord, an attorney named Adolph Rosenbaum who lived at No. 1, Blooms-bury Square, had subjected him to precisely the same sort of annoyance recently suffered by Dr. Dix. For almost a week the Rosenbaum home had been deluged by tradespeople, dinner "guests" and other callers sent thither by bogus letters. Then—again as in the Dix case—there had been a lull of a week or more, after which the annoyances were resumed with such intensity that the Rosenbaums were driven almost mad. They received letters signed "Lord Cholmondeley," saying that seventy guineas was the price of peace. Another item of similarity with Gentleman Joe was the arrival of men from the steamship offices with tickets for St. Petersburg, Cape Town, Calcutta and Hong Kong. The case was solved when Rosenbaum, going to the door to turn away another of his many callers, recognized his former friend Williamson seated at the window of an adjacent house, taking in the scene and laughing so heartily as to bend him double. The *Pall Mall Gazette*, with British reserve, called it "a very extraordinary case."

Peters, being a good fellow, did what he could. But the accused man, who gave his full name and title as Colonel Eugene Edward Fairfax Williamson, appeared before Sir Thomas Henry at Bow Street court and was sentenced to a year at Pentonville Prison. Peters was quite sure that Williamson had taught a Sunday-school class at Trinity Chapel a few years before his London adventure.

1. The attack on the serenity of Dr. Morgan Dix was subtle and mysterious. Some observers (not he) saw artistry in it.

2. Gen. John Adams Dix.

3. Rev. T. DeWitt Talmage.

4. The Herald tells it like it is.

5. Rev. Henry Ward Beecher.

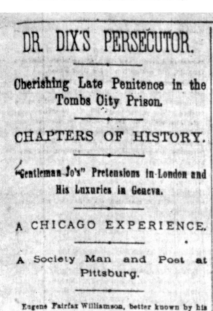

DR. DIX'S PERSECUTOR.

Cherishing Late Penitence in the Tombs City Prison.

CHAPTERS OF HISTORY.

"Gentleman Jo's" Pretensions in London and His Luxuries in Geneva.

A CHICAGO EXPERIENCE.

A Society Man and Poet at Pittsburg.

Eugene Fairfax Williamson, better known by his aliases of "Gentleman Jo" and "High Churchman," left Baltimore by the 11:20 train on Wednesday night, and arrived in this city about seven o'clock yester-

6. Old Trinity Church became a place of stealth, suspicion and other unholy goings-on, thanks to Gentleman Joe's work.

Yours faithfully
Theodore E. Hook

AUTHOR OF "SAYINGS AND DOINGS".

7. Theodore E. Hook, connoisseurs saw, was Gentleman Joe's forerunner—though not his superior—in the delicate art of jokesmanship.

8. In a day of discreet headlines, the Tribune's front-page story (below) was regarded as downright sensational, if no[t] vulgar treatment.

Y, MARCH 20, 1880.

FIFTY CALLS ON DR. DIX

WHAT HIS ENEMY ACCOMPLISHED.

FIFTY PERSONS CALL AT THE HOUSE ON A FO[OL'S] ERRAND—DR. DIX RELIEVED BY THE POST FICE AUTHORITIES—HE REFUSES TO SEE VISITORS—A SECOND LETTER FROM HIS PER[SE] CUTOR—THE DETECTIVES STILL AT WORK.

About fifty persons were sent to the ho[use] of the Rev. Dr. Dix in West Twenty-fifth [Street] yesterday, having received letters asking th[em] to call there upon business of various kin[ds.] They did not see Dr. Dix, but an employé [of] the Post Office Department, who had been s[ent] to the house for the purpose, received th[em] and explained to them that they had been [de] ceived by the person who had been persecut[] ing Dr. Dix for some time before. A sec[ond] letter has been sent by this man to T[HE] TRIBUNE, which is given below. The effo[rts] to trace the author are continued, with ho[pe] of success.

LATEST RESULTS OF THE PLOT.

HOW A LAWYER WHO THOUGHT HE HAD A DIVO[RCE] CASE WAS RECEIVED—PERSONS DESIRING [EM] PLOYMENT MISLED—THE PAPER ON WHICH [THE] NOTES OF "HIGH CHURCHMAN" AND "GENT[LE] MAN JOE" ARE WRITTEN—EFFORTS TO TR[ACE] TH[E] AUTHOR.

True to his promise in the note to THE TRIB[UNE] which was published yesterday, the unknown [per] secutor of the Rev. Dr. Morgan Dix, who signs [him] self variously as "High Churchman" and "G[en] tleman Joe," sent yesterday to Dr. Dix's hous[e a] large number of persons to respond to letter[s pur] porting to have come from the occupant of t[he] house. He said in his note to THE TRIBUNE tha[t he] had sent such letters to "several hundred."

9. James Gordon Bennett.

10. Attorney George Bliss.

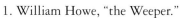

1. William Howe, "the Weeper."

12. The fishy Abraham Hummel.

13. Andrew Carnegie's mother.

14. The wicked Victoria Woodhull.

15. The eight-story Windsor Hotel at Fifth Avenue and 46th Street—here the manager, the Carnegies and other guests of fashion were delighted by the charming Gentleman Joe.

16. The Fifth Avenue Hotel (shown) was another of the swank caravansaries favored by Joe. He usually paid his bills.

7. Despite the removal of the legend, the Windsor Hotel letterhead was the clue that olved the case.

8. You could've toppled Andrew Carnegie ight) with a feather when he learned the attering truth.

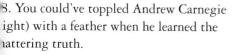

20. District Attorney Phelps

21. Byrnes, Hawkshaw of the force.

21. The noisome Tombs, where the law brought Gentleman Joe's career of luxury and genius to a sad, if deserved, finish.

One can be certain that Captain Byrnes listened to this recital with the growing smile of a man who feels that his troubles are dwindling. A steamfitter before he became a policeman, intelligent but unlearned, he had little interest in literature or in the historical comparison of *modus operandi*. He had paid no attention to the career of Theodore Hook. Otherwise he would have noticed again that Williamson, in the Bloomsbury case, had patterned his style closely after Hook's Berners Street hoax. But Williamson had introduced a new element—the demand for money that seemed a part of the hoax since it was never followed through—just as in the Dix case.

It is difficult to imagine that Byrnes allowed Peters to leave without pumping his hand gratefully. Yet this hot lead cooled suddenly when Dr. Dix, questioned about the matter, said he had not the slightest recollection of Williamson. Still, Dix was so busy with his seven churches that it was not impossible that he would forget a church-school teacher after close to a decade. Byrnes persisted. Peters had mentioned that Williamson had won the acquaintance of the Reverend Dr. Edward Noyes, then of St. Alban's Church. This tip paid off, for Dr. Noyes produced a photograph which Williamson had presented to him. (Williamson, a likable eccentric, was in the habit of presenting even casual friends with gold fountain pens and his photograph.) It showed a man of perhaps thirty-five with a rather handsome face, perfectly groomed Dundreary whiskers and beard, a Puckish smile and lustrous, magnetic eyes. In addition there were the descriptions given by Peters and the clergyman: Williamson was very short, meticulous in dress and had an almost perfect British accent although he was apparently of American birth. His hair and beard were of a rich, reddish brown. He had a ready wit and a personality so engaging that one was apt to place more confidence in him than was justified. Both witnesses stressed that last point. Williamson was so outrageously charming that one felt drawn to him in spite of oneself.

Although he was known for his tenacious memory and attention to detail, Byrnes at this time suffered a momentary fit of absent-mindedness. He entirely forgot to pass on this information about Williamson to Gayler—an omission that placed the Post Office sleuths at a disadvantage, which one could not believe that the captain intended. He did, however, give it to his own men and urge them to hunt down the malefactor, a lover of luxury who frequented expensive hotels.

Meanwhile, Superintendent Gayler, working on the case as if the reputation of the Post Office Department were at stake, had given up on the postcards for the moment and subjected all of Gentleman Joe's sealed letters, of which there were only a few dozen, to close scrutiny. He reasoned that the one mailed in the Fifth Avenue Hotel envelope was virtual proof that the culprit was not staying at the Fifth Avenue. All the other letters were written on plain white paper of the finest quality except that the top edge was rough. Gayler soon hit on the reason. An inch or two had been torn off the top of these sheets, as if along the edge of a ruler. Why should Joe do that? Obviously to eliminate an identifying letterhead, probably that of a hotel. Operatives visited all the better hotels, finding that the paper, in size, watermark and quality, matched that used at the Windsor Hotel, one of the best in town.

This of itself was of little help, since the Windsor had hundreds of guests in addition to Count de Lesseps and the Carnegies. But it happened that another of Gayler's inquiries threw light on this one. Impressed by the ecclesiastical overtones in the case, he had for days been questioning clergymen of the Episcopal and other denominations, asking if they had any theories about the Dix persecution. One minister, an unnamed Presbyterian, recalled that a man named Williamson had once been connected with Trinity Chapel in a minor way, and had left New York under a cloud of some kind. Williamson had made a pledge of $500 to the Presbyterian building fund and had never paid it. The clergyman recalled all this because he had met Williamson on Fifth Avenue a few days earlier. The latter, obviously embarrassed by his failure to pay, excused himself on the ground of his "heavy obligations in Wall Street" but said he would soon make good the pledge. The clergyman's memory of all but the most recent of these details was hazy, but he was positive of the name Williamson, and that was enough.

Thus, through independent investigations, Gayler and Byrnes had hit on the same suspect. The difference was that Gayler, after checking at the Windsor on Saturday afternoon, March nineteenth, was hot on Williamson's trail.

Through a remarkable coincidence, Gayler, whose memory was normally of the steel-trap kind (but who may have been thrown off poise by the excitement of the chase), had an appalling lapse of his own. He quite forgot to notify Captain Byrnes of the new lead. The result was that Byrnes' gumshoes, though seeking the same man, were looking for a needle in a haystack, which one would not like to think was Gayler's intention.

Williamson's signature, in the familiar curlicues of Gentleman Joe, was on the Windsor register twice. He had checked in from Pittsburgh on February fourteenth, shortly before the first epistolary explosion. He had remained there nine days, then had left for a three-week period that coincided precisely with the surcease of the Dix and Buckley afflictions. Once more he had become a Windsor guest on March fourteenth, his stay again coinciding with the new onslaught on Dr. Dix. He had paid his bills and had tipped handsomely. Charles B. Waite, the assistant manager of the Windsor, was convinced that Gayler was making a ghastly mistake. Mr. Williamson, Waite insisted, was genteel, unobtrusive, charming, a descendant of the Virginia Fairfaxes, a friend of wealthy guests at the hotel. "He is the last man who would be engaged in such an affair," Waite said firmly.

In any case, he had checked out at noon on the nineteenth, only a few hours before Gayler and his aides closed in on the Windsor for the kill. He had left no forwarding address but had mentioned that he was going to Baltimore.

NOT IN TIME TO CAPTURE HIM, the *Tribune* headlined excitedly next morning.

Inquiries disclosed that his big, yellow, canvas-covered trunk had indeed been shipped to Baltimore via Dodd's Express, at 944 Broadway. This was disconcerting. Could Waite be right? Criminals were not ordinarily so free-handed about announcing their destinations. Gayler took the express ticket with him (it bore the number 2031) and boarded the next train for Baltimore for all the world like a man who had effaced from his memory any thought of cooperating with Captain Byrnes. Byrnes' men meanwhile were doing a great deal of useless work. Bearing the photograph showing Williamson as of 1870 and wearing Dundreary whiskers (which he had since shaved off), they were visiting hotels in the neighborhood of the rectory in the hope that some clerk would recognize the picture and the name. They had not yet reached the Windsor, which was twenty-one blocks north of the rectory, nor would they ever reach it.

In Baltimore, Gayler conferred with Chief Special Agent David B. Parker, a legendary operative who had maintained mail routes during the Civil War and helped establish new ones to the West Coast since then, and who had come up from Washington to meet him. The two men joined in a canvass of hotels. They spent a full day at this, even checking small rooming houses without finding their man. There was nothing for it but to try to trace the trunk—a formidable task since at the time there were many small local express companies and even more free-lance draymen who would haul anything anywhere for a fee. Gayler hired D. Pinckney West, a Baltimore private detective, to help him in the hunt. Another day was lost in making the rounds of the expressmen before it was learned

THE RECTOR AND THE ROGUE

that the trunk had been hauled by dray not to a hotel but to a private house on the outskirts of town, the home of Michael Heintzman, Jr. at 556 Pennsylvania Avenue.

Quick undercover inquiries disclosed that Heintzman was a prosperous wholesaler of provisions, a business and family man of excellent reputation. Detective West hired a buggy and drove out to the house, a substantial three-story brick dwelling. Admitted by a tall, plump, dark-haired man later found to be Heintzman, West identified himself as an express-company functionary. "A big yellow trunk has been lost," he said. "It seems to have been sent here by mistake."

"Eugene!" Heintzman called. A little man walked in from another room. Barely over five feet tall, with alert eyes and a spade beard of a rich chocolate hue, well trimmed and impeccably tailored, he had about him some of the preposterously bright attractiveness of a toy poodle. "But there is no mistake," he said. "The trunk is my own."

West looked it over with a skeptical expression and after some further parley took his leave. Rejoining Gayler downtown, he informed him that their man was in the house and had better be seized before he moved on. More hours were lost as Gayler wired this intelligence to Colonel Bliss in New York, asking his advice. Bliss hemmed and hawed, fearful that there might be trouble extraditing Williamson from Maryland. Bliss suggested that if he were merely kept under surveillance he might come back to New York of his own accord and could be arrested without danger of legal complications.

Bliss at long last also notified Captain Byrnes, whose feelings can be imagined. All the captain could do was take his men off the case and await developments as they were disclosed by the rival—and forgetful—Post Office operatives.

CHAPTER XI

THE VILLAIN AT BAY

It was all very well for Bliss to say, "Keep him under surveillance." Actually, there was no nearby vantage point from which Gayler and West could watch the brick house without being under surveillance themselves, and how could one prevent a night getaway? Finally Gayler, reasoning that legal technicalities were less frightening than the risk of losing his man entirely, got a warrant and with West knocked at the Heintzman door. This time Williamson himself answered.

"Not the trunk again!" he exclaimed. "It even has my initials on it."

"Not the trunk," Gayler said. "This time it's you. I must place you under arrest, Gentleman Joe."

The little man lost the aplomb so notable in his letters and literally shook with fright. He hardly bothered to glance at the arrest warrant. In a rapid flow of words he admitted everything—the letters to Dr. Dix, to Buckley, Boden, the mayor of Paterson, the Reverend Drs. McKim, Dyer, Rylance and other pastors, the letter to Dr. Swope from Cincinnati, the letters to the hundreds of deluded tradespeople, lawyers, servants, to the department stores and the newspapers—all, all. He sank into a chair, drew out a monogrammed linen handkerchief and mopped his perspiring brow.

"I do not know what in heaven possessed me to do this," he groaned.

Williamson spoke with a clipped British accent. He was the soul of courtesy, giving every sign of a genteel upbringing and an excellent education. A bachelor, he gave his age as thirty-nine and said he was born in Baltimore although he was a member of the Fairfax family of Virginia. For a time after the war he had been a prosperous book dealer in Baltimore, but of late years he had spent much of his time abroad and now had a home in Pittsburgh. He preferred not to name his nearest relatives, he said, until he had cleared himself in this unfortunate matter. He was willing to waive extradition and return to New York only on one condition that he made very distinct—that he be permitted, immediately on arriving, to talk personally with Dr. Dix and beg his forgiveness. If it was possible for him to feel any keener contrition than he did about the trouble he had caused the Dixes, it was about the many servants whose hopes for employment were dashed when they called at the rectory.

"I took the papers every day," he said, "and read the stories they were printing about me. I mixed in the crowd that assembled in front of Dr. Dix's house and enjoyed the joke like the rest of them. The one thing in my conduct that I regret most of all was sending the servants there and disappointing them."

Heintzman, it turned out, was a distant relative with whom Williamson was staying before going on to Chicago—a destination now changed—and who was utterly astonished at the commotion. Williamson presented an interesting picture of real or simulated repentance. There was an expression of puzzlement in his gentle, magnetic eyes. From time to time he shook his head as if in bafflement at his own errant impulses. When Gayler asked him the climactic question—his motive—he extended his hands palms upward in an expression of helplessness.

"You see, that is the point," he said. "I had no motive at all. I have nothing against Dr. Dix or any of these other people."

This was a bit too much for Gayler. As yet he knew nothing about Williamson's earlier troubles in London or at Trinity Chapel, but he did remind the prisoner that one letter had asked the rector for $1,000 and another had raised it to $1,500, which some people might call blackmail or extortion. Williamson fairly recoiled. Such an idea, he said, was totally mistaken. He showed deep reproach that anyone should entertain it. If he had had any such intent, he inquired, would he not have carried it through instead of ignoring the personal addressed to Reddy which invited him to open negotiations? He had not negotiated. He had never intended to negotiate. If he had meant to negotiate, would he have left New York and gone to Baltimore on his way to Chicago? He showed his rail ticket to Chicago. He repeated this argument in several different ways to make certain that Gayler understood the logic of it and would rid himself of the horrid suspicion that there had been so much as a thought of money. Never! The little man was deferent, in fact positively charming, but he was very firm on this point. He was either anxious, or anxious to create the impression that he was anxious, to cooperate in unraveling the puzzle which he personally constituted but which (he said) he could not personally solve.

"I seem to have eccentricities at times," he said, "which are too much for me to understand."

Although he could give no reason why he should have annoyed Dr. Dix, he was fertile with suggestions that, whatever the reason, there was no criminal intent. He cited the fact that he had written similar letters to Buckley and many others without any mention of money. This, he felt, was further proof that there was no idea of gain in his letter-writing—quite the contrary, since he had spent a good deal for postage, not to mention the effort expended, and the whole project represented a financial loss to him.

"But if you had nothing against Dr. Dix," Gayler asked, "then how did you happen to hit on his name?"

"Well, I am a High Churchman," Williamson said earnestly, "and I suppose it's likely that Dr. Dix's name occurred to me simply because he is the leading High Churchman. I'm sure that's all there is to it. As for Buckley, I happened to ride past his saloon on the horse car. I saw his shingle and thought he ought to send money to the *Herald* for Irish relief. You see how it went."

When Gayler asked if he would make a written confession, he said he was perfectly willing but was so nervous that his hands shook and he had lost his customary facility with the pen. He would dictate the statement, he said. He no longer appeared *that* nervous. Gayler felt that he was probably using this stratagem to reserve his liberty to repudiate the statement should this later prove to be to his advantage. The Post Office investigator later admitted that he had never encountered so fascinating and yet so puzzling a man in his life. Gayler wrote as Williamson dictated:

> I, Eugene Fairfax Williamson, freely and voluntarily confess that I was the author of the annoying postal cards and letters which were recently posted and delivered in New-York.... I do not know what caused me to do this. Dr. Dix has never injured me, nor have any of the other persons who were annoyed by my wicked acts.... I solemnly declare I did not intend to extort money from Dr. Dix or any other person, and did not even answer the personal which was put in the *Herald* in reply to one of my letters.
>
> I am going to New-York voluntarily with Mr. Gayler and Mr. West, and I earnestly beg the forgiveness of all whom I have annoyed by my misconduct.
>
> —E. Fairfax Williamson
> Baltimore, Mar. 24, 1880. Witness: D. Pinckney West.

Before leaving, Gayler spoke aside with Heintzman, who said he had known Williamson only since the late War Between the States. Williamson had told him also that his home was in Pittsburgh, he said, but he traveled a great deal and Heintzman was apt to get pleasant postcards from him from New York, St. Louis or Europe. He did not know how Williamson lived in such style. He must either have inherited money or he was well paid for his literary labors, for he did not seem to be regularly employed. "He is a devoted churchman," Heintzman said, "and has written several books on religious subjects. He has a fine tenor voice and often breaks out with a hymn." Heintzman admitted that he found it hard to believe that Williamson had done those odd things in New York even though he confessed them. He was, Heintzman conceded, eccentric, but talented, friendly and accommodating.

Indeed, Heintzman shook his guest's hand warmly and wished him luck as the detectives took him away. His left wrist was handcuffed to West's right, an arrangement he protested at once. He was excruciatingly sensitive about the vulgarities connected with arrest. He argued that a Fairfax's word was his bond, and even made a pale joke about it, suggesting how ridiculous it appeared for him to carry a walking stick in one hand while the other was handcuffed. West finally put away the manacles, since the prisoner seemed not only non-aggressive but non-athletic, but tapped his pistol inside his coat meaningly.

Gayler questioned Williamson further about his motive when they reached the Baltimore police headquarters. The little man knit his brows and pondered. "I suppose it may have been a practical joke," he said in the manner of a man in utter ignorance who is making a wild guess. He was, he said, a direct descendant of the first Fairfax in this country, Thomas Fairfax, sixth baron of Cameron. This Fairfax had inherited most of northern Virginia—everything between the Rappahannock and the Potomac, some six million acres.

He was a dear friend of George Washington until Washington outraged him by turning rebel. Being an unreconstructed Tory, Fairfax was not as lucky as Trinity Parish in keeping his proprietorship, which was taken by the State of Virginia after the war. Williamson, in keeping with such a background, told of having served as a colonel in the Confederate army. He was now a communicant of St. Andrew's Church in Pittsburgh, a member of the choir and a close friend of the rector, to whom he had dedicated one of his books. Oh, yes, he said, he was an author and poet in a modest way. The reason he gave for his two stays at the Windsor Hotel was simply that he liked to get around, being particularly fond of New York, and he also wanted to see his friends, the Carnegies, who lived at the Windsor. During the interval between his two stays at the hotel, he had returned to Pittsburgh.

"I wanted to discuss a new book with my publisher," he said, "and I also wanted to take my place in the choir for a Sunday service at dear St. Andrew's. Then too, I am a newspaperman by way of a hobby. I cover social events at my leisure for the *Post* in Pittsburgh. I turned in some rather good copy if I do say so."

Gayler, as he described it afterward, felt that Williamson had the kind of magnetism found in such platform orators as Robert Ingersoll or James Blaine—an ability to kindle actual affection on the part of listeners as well as to command their interest. One had to be careful while in his company or one would begin to like him. He had a quality usually described as hypnotic but which really consisted of nothing more than an attractive combination of characteristics—perfect courtesy, a warm smile, a mellifluous voice, the diction and persuasiveness of a highly educated man, an innate attitude of friendliness along with every social grace, and all this expressed by the eager little face over the perfectly tailored body. One had frequently to remind oneself that he was either a liar and scoundrel or a madman.

In New York, it was apparent that the news that the forger had been arrested and had confessed brought an odd sense of regret to reporters whose lives he had lightened. As Gentleman Joe he had been vintage champagne. As Williamson, in the ordinary course of news spoilage, he would soon be small beer. Just as a jigsaw puzzle's fascination is gone the moment it is pieced together, so is the public interest in a figure of mystery once his mystery has vanished. Now, journalistically, it seemed only a matter of polishing off Gentleman Joe—drawing together the few mournful loose ends remaining before the inevitable punishment that would end the case and finish him as a news commodity. According to word from Baltimore, in his guise as Williamson he was pathetic rather than heroic, a popinjay scared silly, yet the windiest liar since Munchausen, making such claims as being a Fairfax, an author and a friend of the Carnegies.

Captain Byrnes' information that Williamson had once been dismissed from Trinity Chapel seemed to take care of the question of motive. A group of reporters who visited the chapel found that he had taught a Sunday-school class there for two years, from 1869 to 1871. At that time he had described himself as a Wall Street broker, which he was not. He had been an excellent teacher. His dismissal came about because of one of those scandals which newspapers at the time were forbidden to describe specifically and which they termed "improper conduct" and evaded with other euphemisms implying that he had attempted some indecency with boys in the junior choir.

So *that* was why Dix had fired him, causing the grudge. But this theory crumbled when it developed that the rector had had nothing to do either with Williamson's appointment as a teacher or his dismissal. In fact, he still could not remember the man. Dr. Swope, who had been in charge of the chapel in 1871, as he was now, was the man who had swung the axe. He would have seemed the logical target for revenge, if that was in Williamson's mind. Yet Dr. Swope had received only one bogus postcard—the one from Cincinnati—whereas Dix had been the beneficiary of hundreds.

Andrew Carnegie and his mother, interviewed at the Windsor, told of their acquaintance with Williamson. They had met him at whist parties in Pittsburgh, Mrs. Carnegie said in her Scottish burr, and he seemed to move in the best society—two statements that might have been considered redundant in the money-oriented aristocracy of the time. She described Williamson as cultivated and popular, friendly with everybody, the author of several volumes of poetry and drama. She recalled that he had presented her with three volumes of his writings at a time when they were only slightly acquainted, yet he had done it so gracefully that she was charmed. He had mentioned his relationship with the Fairfaxes. According to the *Tribune*, "Mrs. Carnegie said she could only account for this writing of letters by Mr. Williamson on the ground of a monomania taking that form." The Carnegies could not have been more astonished had their good friend Matthew Arnold been discovered as a voyeur. While Williamson was at the Windsor they had dined with him and joined him in card-playing groups, always enjoying his company. There had been considerable discussion about the mysterious visitations on Dr. Dix—talk into which he entered with his usual keenness. The Carnegies did not know that Williamson had any occupation other than his writing and assumed that he inherited some of the Fairfax wealth. They had not yet been told of his earlier difficulties at Trinity Chapel and were inclined to sympathize with him as the victim of an aberration which was annoying enough, to be sure, but never dangerous and not without amusement.

It was discovered that his five books, all small volumes, had been published from 1876 to 1879 by the Stevenson & Foster Company of Pittsburgh. They included four religious dramas: *Sylvia's Jubilee*, *Miriam*, *The Sisters of Alhambra* and *Little Golden Hair*, the latter for children. The fifth contained two poems on sacred subjects, "The Annunciation" and "The Nativity." Several had been warmly praised by critics in Pittsburgh, Baltimore and New York. The New York

Tribune had said in small part of his poetic drama, *Miriam*, "Mr. Williamson deserves an undoubted place in the front rank of our new poets," adding a laudation which could as well be applied to his letters written under the *nom de plume* of Gentleman Joe: "He writes with almost faultless melody... and with a simplicity which proves his possession of an imagination as trained as it is rich and vivid." The *World* had said of another volume, "Those who have read Mr. Williamson's 'Miriam' will hardly need to be told that this new volume from his pen is beautiful—he has the happy art of talking to the young in 'Little Golden Hair,' and he carries them with him by the tender sympathy of his heart.... The manner in which this little fairy story is given cannot fail of making a healthy moral impression on the young mind." The *Herald*, which evidently had not reviewed any of the Williamson books at the time of their publication, now said of one of them, "'The Sisters of Alhambra' had quite a sale here, and is really well written and contains some passages not unworthy of Dion Boucicault."

No longer was there any talk of Williamson's waning newsworthiness on the part of the men of the press. Not every day did they encounter a globe-trotter, a dramatist and poet, a society man, friend of the Carnegies and moralist for the young, who turned his talents in the odd directions taken by Gentleman Joe. He had a trait beloved of journalists, the quality of a continued story so helpful for circulation. Just when his interest seemed played out he could bring other glittering facets of singularity into view. Had a full-length biography of E. Fairfax Williamson's entire thirty-nine years been available just then, it would have enjoyed a brisk sale. The newsmen did their best to supply one, sending requests to correspondents in Pittsburgh, Baltimore, Richmond and London for more, more about Williamson. Reporters hurried to Buckley's saloon with word of the forger's arrest and asked if the name meant anything to him.

"I never heard of him," Buckley said. He added thoughtfully, "And do you know, I don't want to."

CHAPTER XII

GENIUS BEHIND BARS

Williamson's touching but illogical hope to keep his misdoings unknown to his family and his family unknown to the press was quickly
blasted. The *Herald* published an excited dispatch from Pittsburgh:
"Eugene Fairfax Williamson, who was arrested for attempting to
black-mail Rev. Morgan Dix, is one of the best known society men
in this city, and the news of his connection with the Dix affair created a perfect furore." He came from a fine old Southern family, the
Herald went on, of which his own branch in late years had settled in
Pittsburgh. His older brother Alfred was the wealthy vice president
of the huge National Tube Company. His older sister Alicia was the
wife of G. F. Bailey, owner of the Bailey Reflector Company. His
seventy-five-year-old widowed mother lived with the Baileys. The
Williamsons and the Baileys were welcome guests in some of the
grandest homes in town. E. Fairfax Williamson himself maintained
a small but luxurious bachelor apartment on Fifth Avenue in that
city and was noted for his collection of figurines from France and

Italy, and music boxes from Switzerland and Germany. St. Andrew's, of which he was a prominent member and valued tenor, was the most fashionable Episcopal church in the city, very High. He had an extensive knowledge of sacred music, and in fact had been attending the musicians' convention in Cincinnati when he wrote the single bogus letter to Dr. Swope. He had been a groomsman at the wedding of his good friend the Reverend Dr. Reese Alsop, rector of St. Andrew's, who was reported to have said, "I cannot believe this of Eugene." Williamson had served as an usher at the consecration of Bishop Riley in Pittsburgh and was elected a lay deputy to the recent diocesan convention held at Meadville and to other church assemblies held at Erie and Philadelphia. As the Pittsburgh *Commercial Gazette* put it, "Hon. Ormsby Phillips, an official at St. Andrew's church, said [Williamson]... attended punctiliously to every church duty.... He seemed to have the most profound respect—amounting almost to adoration—for the Rector, Rev. Mr. Alsop, who had been especially kind to him during a protracted illness." A confirmed collector, "he also had the autograph of every Bishop of his church in the United States and hundreds of dignitaries in foreign lands—in most cases the autograph accompanying a photograph."

He was believed to be independently wealthy, with interesting eccentricities. "He quite frequently 'dropped into poetry,'" the *Gazette* went on, "and in several of our home papers his stanzas found a place—being generally much above the average." He wrote society news for the Pittsburgh *Post* on space rates (just for fun, it was thought). He had recently contributed a host of jottings from New York and had covered a few lavish Fifth Avenue gatherings as if he had been one of the guests, which he had not, having gotten his facts from friends at the Windsor and by judicious cribbing from the New York papers—a common journalistic practice and not frowned upon when one's thefts were used in another city. He had included many items about his fellow guests at the Windsor, the Carnegies and

Count de Lesseps, and about himself as well, for he obviously put himself in the same social category. The news of his arrest so stunned the Pittsburgh élite that they felt there must be some mistake. True, he loved to write letters. He had a habit of disappearing without warning from Pittsburgh, after which his friends there would ultimately receive gay and amusing missives from him wherever he happened to be, in this country or Europe.

"His lavishness in making presents," said the *Herald*, "amounted almost to as much of a mania as his passion for music boxes. He was constantly bestowing costly gifts upon his acquaintances. He gave diamond pins, gold watches and similar articles to the young people he knew, and he kept his young lady friends supplied with hothouse flowers."

When a substantial citizen is caught in a crime, it is customary for the press to review more closely his past activities and discover that he was a villain all along. The *Gazette* sniffed conscientiously but could detect nothing malodorous about Williamson's life in Pittsburgh, admitting in a headline, PROMINENT PEOPLE ASSERT THAT, WITH AMPLE OPPORTUNITIES, HE NEVER PLAYED THE KNAVE. It sent a reporter out to the Locust Street home of the Baileys to interview his elderly mother. It must be borne in mind that at this time Mrs. Williamson knew nothing about any past illegalities committed by her son, nor (if she herself was aware of his inversion) did she know that it was known in New York. She gave the interview under the impression that the only thing against him was his bedevilling of Dr. Dix. Her son had been brilliant and somewhat unstable since boyhood, she said—bookish, musical, fluent in French and German. "We have always considered him as very erratic," she went on, "and since he was quite a boy he has had a perfect mania for playing tricks, and always has been a great lover of fun.... When his brother Alfred read the intelligence... he says that he both laughed and cried, first on account of the ridiculousness of sending all these people to Dr. Dix's home on a myriad different errands, and then at the disgrace it cast upon Eugene. The only explanation that we can give is that he has been overcome by an uncontrollable mania."

When Williamson reached New York in Gayler's custody on March twenty-fifth, he was followed by swarms of reporters as he was hustled to Postmaster James' office for questioning by postal and police officials and an assistant district attorney. Although Captain Byrnes' men had been outdistanced at the finish by the Post Office investigators, the captain was present, determined not to be elbowed out of the limelight now by a parcel of amateurs.

Williamson seems to have entered the conference with mistaken optimism, feeling that his bargaining position was strong. Through no fault of Gayler's, who had known nothing of his checkered background, Williamson had thought that the darker episodes of his past were still secret and that the only known blemish was his letter-writing escapade as Gentleman Joe. He had high confidence in his eloquence and histrionic skill. His good record in Pittsburgh and the warm reception of his published works would help him. He evidently felt sure that the proper blend of candor and contrition would persuade the rector and the district attorney to forgive what after all could be construed as mere horseplay.

Alas, the chill that seized him when he discovered the truth must have set him to shaking again. Too much, far too much, was known about him. The hoax on Rosenbaum was known in every detail, as was the year he spent in an English prison. Perhaps even more damaging was that almost-suppressed little scandal with the choir boy at Trinity Chapel in 1871. Always the actor, he had counted on playing the sympathetic role of the propitiatory prodigal whose one transgression could be indulged. Instead he was exposed as a criminal, jailbird and pervert. His role had been ruined and yet there was none other for him to play. Gentleman Joe walked on a stage where he had expected some compassion, to find his script in shreds and his audience pelting him with eggs and fruit. The agreement that he be allowed to state his case to Dr. Dix was kept. Reporters pleaded to be permitted to witness the confrontation between the two principals—a meeting of Episcopalians of similar ecclesiastical beliefs that promised to be of secular interest—but had to wait outside. This was Holy Thursday, with Easter only three days away. The rector had a thousand things on his mind, including a service at Trinity Church under his personal direction, but he left an assistant minister in charge and hurried to the Post Office. It was seen that his mouth formed that familiar straight line as he slipped through the wings to enact his own role, that of avenging righteousness.

Colonel Bliss had already had a long talk with the little man, who impressed him by (a) his willingness to confess his own letter-writing, and (b) his eagerness to portray it as mischievous, even wicked, but never prompted by sordid or illegal motives. In the midst of it, Williamson seemed so attracted to Bliss that he pulled from his waistcoat an expensive-looking watch and chain and offered them to him as a gift. The colonel declined them. He later said he felt that Williamson might have a small "bee in his bonnet" but that he was unquestionably sane in the bare legal definition of the word, meaning simply that he knew right from wrong. "I think you may say," Bliss went on, "he is penitent like the case of when the devil was sick, the devil a monk would be, but when the devil was well, the devil a monk was he."

Williamson made no offer of jewelry to Dr. Dix, but spoke with him earnestly. Each reported later on this conversation as follows:

Dr. Dix: "I did not recognize Williamson at first, but when he told me that he taught in the Chapel Sunday school nine years ago, I recalled him. He got into trouble for a crime so horrible that I don't like to tell it.... He [now] asked for mercy and said he would leave the country and change his name. He mentioned stoutly that he had no intention of levying black-mail, not expecting to get a dollar from anyone. I see no possible motive. He is either a great scoundrel or he is insane. As to the question of insanity, that is for the experts to determine. He seems to possess much intelligence, and has written and published poetry. He says that he never visited saloons or drank. He seems to have selected by chance the names of persons to whom he sent letters and postal cards. He tells me that he took some of them from signs as he rode in the street cars.... I found him full of regret at being in the hands of the law and he earnestly implored my forgiveness, but that is not penitence. Penitence is a religious word, and would imply when used by a clergyman a sincere sorrow for sin. I did not find this man in that condition."

Williamson: "The Doctor was very polite to me, but he couldn't be otherwise than that, you know.... He asked me if I had anything against him and I told him no. Lord bless me, how could I have anything against the good Dr. Dix? He was my old pastor, and I wouldn't harm him for the world.... He was reserved and polite. He is cold, very cold, like his father."

Williamson was booked on charges of forgery and attempted extortion. For all his brave front he was pale as he was assigned the same cell in the Tombs that had once been occupied by another mad brain, George Francis Train. The Tombs, so called because of its gray granite construction and its oppressive gloom, was the city detention cooler for prisoners unable to raise bail before trial. It was a place so sordid that even newspapermen were revolted by it. One of them, Junius Henri Browne, in his *The Great Metropolis*, wrote, "The prisoners are locked up in their cells during the night and much of the day, but are permitted to take exercise, and go through the farce of getting 'fresh air,' in the galleries at certain hours. 'Fresh air' indeed! The atmosphere of the Tombs is as vicious materially as it is morally. It is foul, even poisonous, and enough to breed a pestilence. Most of the prisoners are hardened and degraded creatures.... The police strike me as unpleasantly as the criminals; for familiarity has made them callous, and they laugh and jeer at degradation which is revolting, and at misery which is too deep for tears."

Williamson, the *bon vivant*, quailed at the prospect of continued residence in this unlovely place. Before he was locked in his cell the reporters at last had their innings with him. They found him a hard one to pin down. In one breath he went into detail about his letter-writing and in the next he implied doubt that he had written any letters at all.

"Just remember this," he said, "that I'm very sorry for whatever has occurred, no matter who has done it.... I haven't said that I wrote the letters, you know. Of course you know who wrote them, but please remember that I don't say I did it. I can't understand it at all. There must be something weak up here [touching his forehead]. I have a passion for writing. Not now, but generally [looking furtively at the reporter]. I like to sit right down and write a lot of stuff... and I tell you I am a pretty good writer. This mania has ruined me now socially. My trouble in London would not have been known here but for this new trouble, and now all my friends will go back on me. I don't know what prompted me to do it—remember I have not said that I did it—but I have not been well at all since I had typhoid fever about three years ago."

He seemed in the predicament of being quite proud of his exploits, anxious on the one hand to get proper credit for them and fearful on the other hand of suffering punishment for the illegality that accompanied the credit. He was an incessant reader, he said. In London years earlier he had spent much time at the British Museum. He had enjoyed the novels and verse of Theodore Hook, but even more so Hook's practical jokes, particularly the one on Mrs. Tottenham. Thus he showed integrity in giving Hook due honor as the inventor, at the same time implying (without really saying) that he had improved on Hook in some respects. When asked if he had indeed had the nerve to witness the last "raid" on Dr. Dix, when the servants and divorce lawyers called, he nodded and explained with typical guile:

"Well, I saw in the papers that something was going to happen at Dr. Dix's house that day, and it was very natural that I should go with the rest of the people to see the fun. I was there. Do you remember how it snowed and rained?... You didn't see me then, I suppose? I walked the Square, in Twenty-fifth-street, Sixth-avenue, and Twenty-sixth-street, all the morning, and I saw lots of visitors call on the Doctor. I couldn't stay after 12 o'clock, though I wanted to. I had to go to Baltimore on the 1 o'clock train, and I went."

(He was prone to factual unreliability even when this was unnecessary, for it was Friday when he watched the rectory and Saturday when he left for Baltimore.)

He gladly explained his Fairfax lineage, although the explanation left his listeners more confused than ever. His grandmother on his father's side, he said, was the daughter of George William Fairfax, a nephew of Thomas Fairfax, the sixth baron, and was a member of the direct English branch. There were two English branches, he added, and the title of the house now rested in John Cantree Fairfax, a physician residing in Brandenburg, Prince Georges County, Maryland. The latter could, if he wished, use his title as the eleventh baron. Williamson said he had never met him but had been very friendly with his predecessor, the late Charles Fairfax of Baltimore, and had always been acknowledged as a relative. "It would be the height of absurdity," he said, "for me to profess to be anything but what I am."

(That last remark was subject to conflicting interpretations. In any case, Dr. John Cantree Fairfax as well as several members of the family in Virginia denied that they had ever heard of Williamson and said that if he was a relative it must be in a sense similar to the universal relationship to Adam. Newspapermen, diverted by his one-sided family pride, took to referring to him among themselves as Lord Fairfax, or simply The Lord.)

Williamson was more cautious when informed that Confederate officers had written from Baltimore that there was no record that he had been a colonel or had been given a commission of any rank.

"I wasn't in the army proper," he said, "and I don't know as I ought to state just what my services were—that is, not here at the North. I have lived here at the North a long time, and my views have changed a great deal. I don't have the same feelings that I used to have."

"Are you entitled to the rank of colonel?"

"No, I am not properly; my friends gave me that. You know how it is at the South. I was a lieutenant, and a brevet captain, and my friends made me a brevet colonel."

As the *Times* man put it, "Williamson here returned to his cell, leaving his visitor with the conviction that he is either, as he claims, slightly unbalanced in his mind, or that he is an actor who displays consummate art in the role of a lunatic."

The growing throng of New Yorkers who had become interested in Hookiana felt that Williamson was every bit as sane as Hook, that he was indeed a latter-day follower—as brilliant as Hook and in some ways better. After the smashing success of Hook's Berners Street hoax of 1810 there had been numerous feeble imitations in London and other English cities—even a few in Paris and one in Berlin. Hook himself wrote in annoyance, "Copy the joke and it ceases to *be* one—any fool can imitate an example once set." The cult eventually had died out entirely. There had been an interval of many years, not as long but as gloomy as the Dark Ages, when no such hoax had been perpetrated and the art seemed lost. Now, thanks to Williamson and the unknown beguiler of Mrs. Otis in Boston, there had been a renaissance in the New World. True, Williamson's 1873 flimflam of Rosenbaum had taken place in London, and yet birth and blood were what counted. England could no more claim that

enterprise than it could Whistler's Mother. Even a cursory study of
the Rosenbaum work made it plain that for all its several refine-
ments it really constituted practice and rehearsal for the Dix-et-al
masterwork of 1879–80. Hook himself, typically contradicting
his own words, had sharpened his skills with just such a rehearsal.
In 1809, a year before Berners Street, he had confounded a Covent
Garden apothecary by sending him scores of wagonloads of bricks,
hay, lumber, toys and many other things. Certainly Berners Street
would never have been the triumph it was without this comparatively humble effort in Covent Garden behind it.

It seemed evident that good jokesmanship usually was accompanied by moral failings of one kind or another which one accepted
good-naturedly as one did the soprano with the divine voice and
shrewish temper. Hook was hardly more an angel than Williamson. Born in 1788, he was the grandson of an Anglican clergyman
and the son of a musician and composer. Precocity and exuberance
ran in the family. When his older brother entered him at Oxford,
the grave Vice Chancellor asked the usual question about religion:
"Are you prepared to sign the Thirty-Nine Articles?" Theodore
replied briskly, "Oh yes, sir—forty if you please." Naturally he was
not long at Oxford. He wrote his first play at fourteen—an execrable
farce that was nevertheless produced—and thereafter he turned out
play after play between escapades that made him the talk of London.
Slim, handsome, improvident, he became much in demand socially
because any party he attended was sure to be a success. He could
improvise sidesplitting rhymes at the piano for the whole guest list.
He so impressed the Prince Regent (later George IV) that he made
Hook treasurer of the island of Mauritius, a £2,000-a-year post.
This was a mistake. The irresponsible Hook applied himself only to
gaming and horse-racing and seems to have been astonished when
his accounts were found to be £12,000 short. Although the evidence
suggests that the embezzlement was the work of an underling, Hook

THE RECTOR AND THE ROGUE

was blamed and brought back to England in disgrace. Constantly in debt, he thereafter became an editor, writer and famous tosspot. He produced a dozen popular novels of surprising merit considering that each was written practically overnight, between convivialities and with creditors hounding him. Although the one-time cock of the walk had become a bit raffish, he was still a party-enlivener and friend of Coleridge, Sheridan and Byron. When he died at 53 in 1841, he was in debt to the enormous sum of £30,000—itself a triumph of a sort, since no one else would have been able to impose on lenders to such an amount.

All this was a delight to those bookworms looking for antecedents. Not only had Williamson drawn inspiration from Hook but the two were cast in the same mold, to judge from their similarities of character and habit, of literary and musical bent, and general unreliability. Perhaps their greatest resemblance (outside of their turn for humor) lay in their passion to be in the public eye. Neither was happy unless he was creating a sensation. On one occasion, when Hook was touring Wales by carriage with his friend the actor Charles Mathews, Hook suddenly complained, "The scenery is all very fine, but nobody looks at us; the thing is getting a little dull." He bought a box of large black wafers, carefully affixed them to their white steed in the geometrically regular design applied to rockinghorses and thereafter drew the attention of all Welshmen.

CHAPTER XIII

THE CONFEDERATE AGENT

As Warden James Finn locked Williamson in his cell, he did a double-take. "Haven't I seen you before?" he inquired. Williamson uneasily denied that he had the pleasure of recalling Finn's acquaintance. Finn searched his memory. It was The Lord's British accent—a rarity in the Tombs—that seemed to recall a meeting in the past. Sure enough, he consulted the records and discovered that Williamson had briefly been a non-paying guest there five years earlier. On May 14, 1875, when he was living at 132 East Thirty-fourth Street, he had been arrested on a charge of molestation made by a callous Western Union messenger boy known to be capable of blackmail. Released on $500 bail, he had jumped bail and skipped town. Thus he was still technically a fugitive from justice.

It was this second report of a scrape involving boys (along with Dr. Dix's revulsion from describing the "horrible crime" of 1871) that made plain the nature of one of Williamson's many eccentricities. But inversion was so unmentionable in 1880 that only the more knowing readers would have understood unless they had read all of the widely separated clues. Even newspapermen, who were of course hardened to all manner of debauchery, were said to be revolted by sexual aberration. The fact that they continued to treat Williamson with front-page prominence and with good humor showed the impact of his charm as well as his attainments.

Nevertheless, given the mores of the day, his homosexuality made it impossible for him to get a fair trial. Polite society's attitude toward the phenomenon was compounded of ignorance and intolerance. The clergy of course was agreed that it was synonymous with depravity. Ironically, Dr. Dix knew of it not only through experience in this and doubtless other cases but also because of his definitive knowledge of the history of Trinity Parish. Edward Hyde, Viscount Cornbury—a cousin of Queen Anne—had been governor of New York, 1702–08, and in 1705 had granted a lease by which Trinity came into possession of one of its parcels of crown land. Cornbury's collection of silk dresses was the scandal of the day, and "there were stories of his wooing soldiers from his balcony while dressed in women's garb." Dr. Dix's remark about Williamson's crime being "so horrible that I don't like to tell it," published in every New York paper, was a crushing indictment because of its very evasion. The little man stood convicted by a leading divine of conduct so atrocious that it could not even be described.

This intolerance had another effect. It so shamed Williamson's family that thenceforth, although they supported him in a somewhat covert way, they did not bail him out of the Tombs nor, with a lone exception, did they visit New York to encourage him. Even more damaging from the point of view of historians scratching for information about the great hoaxer, the Williamson family thereafter shut their doors to reporters. Dr. Dix thus must bear much of the blame for the many areas of ignorance that plague us today in appraising Williamson's career—ignorance which it seems no amount of scholarship will ever dissolve.

According to his own story, he was educated at a Baltimore seminary and sent abroad at seventeen to matriculate at the University of Paris. As a true Fairfax, however, he rushed home at the outbreak of the Civil War. Fragments of information that now poured in as a result of his arrest pictured him as a poseur of marvelous persistence who had flitted about the world ever since, leaving a murky trail of doubt, misunderstanding and disagreement. In 1862, when he was twenty-one, he had been collared in Baltimore, accused of secretly trying to form a Confederate cavalry regiment. The arrested rebel cavalrymen, on the other hand, called him a traitor and said that he had betrayed them to the federal authorities. This instance of his being accused by both sides was typical of his capacity for fooling everyone and spreading utter confusion—a field in which even Hook partisans had to admit that Williamson was far superior. He wriggled out of the Baltimore difficulty, perhaps because one charge tended to throw doubt on the other. He next turned up in London in a natty Confederate uniform, calling himself Major E. Fairfax Williamson and saying he was an aide of the society-loving General "Prince John" Magruder and was in England on a highly confidential mission for the Confederacy. To others he mentioned privately that he was right-hand man for the Virginian John Murray Mason, the Confederate envoy who was then being treated so coolly by the British. Renting handsome lodgings in the West End, he attended Anglican services and mingled in good society. He wrote friends in Baltimore that he was paying court to a British girl of noble lineage—a girl it was safest now to assume was a fiction. He let it be known that he was a Fairfax and that although his family had dropped its claim to the peerage since the Revolution, he intended to prove and assume his rightful title as Lord Fairfax.

This of course required that he renounce his American (Confederate) citizenship, a thing he said he could never do while his home-land was fighting for its existence. He would wait until the

Confederacy was triumphant—a consummation he devoutly hoped to help bring about with his own efforts—before he would cross the ocean again to claim his English heritage.

He avoided the official Confederate envoys then in London. These gentlemen became aware of him because of the splash he made in society and also because of his weakness for distributing his photographs in uniform. They were dubious because he seemed to be doing nothing at all for the Confederacy and also because "there was something wrong in the details of the uniform." He often went down to Oxford to foregather with a group of Southern blades—the sons of wealthy planters—attending college there. Generous as always, he handed out among them gifts such as fountain pens and cufflinks of good quality. One of them, however, Frank Corbin of Virginia, who was acquainted with some of the Fairfaxes, was skeptical about his connection with that family. Word came across the ocean of his earlier arrest in Baltimore and the feeling grew that he must be a Northern spy.

These mounting suspicions restricted the major's social life enough so that in 1863 he left England (General Lee needed him, he said) and dropped out of sight for five years. Williamson now filled in part of that interval. He said he had sailed on the *City of Manchester* bearing secret dispatches and was arrested as a Confederate spy when he reached New York. A quantity of worthless letters and papers was found in his pockets and was taken from him. The real dispatches, sewn into the soles of his shoes, escaped detection, but he was sent as a prisoner of war to Fort Hamilton in Brooklyn. Later he was transferred to Fort McHenry in Baltimore, and from there to the Old Capitol Prison in Washington, where he said he suffered great privation. Finally he was moved to Fortress Monroe in Virginia before he was regularly exchanged in 1864 as a prisoner of war.

(A review of these arrests in New York, however, suggested that his Fairfax memory was imperfect, for his name was not listed among them. The records at Fort Hamilton and Fort McHenry disclosed that he had never been detained at either place. In dealing with The Lord, his questioners found, it was best to have corroborating information.)

The next corroborating information showed that he surfaced briefly in St. Louis in 1868, then in Chicago the following year. Here he joined the congregation at the Episcopal Cathedral, told of his Fairfax lineage and worked so enthusiastically for the church that many wondered why he did not take holy orders. To this he always replied that he felt he could do God's work more good by his labors, his financial aid and his influence as a layman.

It was while he was there that High Church Bishop Henry John Whitehouse of Illinois began his bloody canonical duel with the Low Church Reverend Dr. Charles Edward Cheney, rector of Christ Church in Chicago—a quarrel that began, strange to say, because of Dr. Cheney's practice of omitting the prescribed word "regenerate" from the baptismal service. The bishop said the rector must use the word. The rector declined, accusing the bishop of "unprotestantizing" the church. In the long struggle for God's blessing that followed, the bishop did his best to depose the rector while the rector strove to unseat the bishop. Episcopalians all over the nation took sides, cheering for one and abusing the other. The battle ended in something of a draw, neither being able to unfrock the other and the rector still refusing to say "regenerate"—an unhappy situation Dr. Cheney ultimately resolved by resigning voluntarily and founding the Reformed Episcopal Church. Williamson was said to have made a close study of the case. High Churchman that he was, he became friendly with Bishop Whitehouse and offered him his support.

But he never stayed long in one place, either because of wanderlust or because he was apt to make claims that it was hard even for a Fairfax to fulfill. He had luxurious rooms, carelessly gave away fountain pens, watches and small jewelry, and seemed to be wealthy.

Yet he never gave the church the enormous donation that he said he had in mind.

Late in 1869 he was in New York, attaching himself to Trinity Chapel with pious fervor. Since he always made it a point to introduce himself to the pastor and to discuss recondite questions of theology and liturgy, Dr. Swope soon became acquainted with him and gave him a Sunday-school class. Swope, like Dr. Dix, was of course wholly on Bishop Whitehouse's side and pleased with Williamson's intelligent support of the bishop. A native of Maryland, Swope was also keenly aware of the Fairfaxes and delighted to have so amiable a member of the clan in his fold—delighted also at Williamson's talk of making a substantial gift of money. On one occasion Williamson found in a pew an opened letter addressed to a lady communicant. Its contents were calculated to cloud her reputation a trifle. Williamson, gallant Fairfax that he was, made haste to suppress it in order to protect her. (It was now believed that he wrote it himself.)

An omnivorous reader, he often bought books at a store owned by Frank Leseur at Twenty-ninth and Broadway, across from the swank Gilsey House where Williamson was living at the time. Well read in the Oxford Movement and the Tractarians, he also liked Balzac, Charles Lever and Byron and had a special passion for Theodore Hook. He seemed to have read all of Hook's novels and verse—he could quote paragraphs and stanzas with ease—in addition to having studied his life. He admired Hook's lightning wit, his ability to make jokes or puns even at his own expense; as when he was temporarily immured for debt and a visiting friend remarked that at any rate he had a pleasant cell. Hook agreed, "So it is, barring the windows." Williamson said he was a Wall Street speculator, mentioned casually his friendship with such manipulators as Commodore Vanderbilt and Daniel Drew, and told of killings in railroad and manufacturing securities. He did it for amusement and to add to his donations to the church, he said; being a Fairfax, he did not need the money himself. Since he always seemed at leisure and enjoyed chess, Leseur took him on during quiet hours in the store. Williamson had a 'possum style at chess. He seemed negligent and inattentive as he talked pleasantly of his exploits or sang snatches from "Sun of My Soul, Thou Saviour Dear," or "Praise to the Holiest in the Height." He knew scores of hymns faultlessly. Leseur would build up his attack to the point where he was poised for the next move, when he expected to slaughter his opponent with a quick checkmate. He was invariably beside himself with vexation when he discovered that Williamson was doing that very thing to him a move in advance. But the little man was always agreeable. Leseur often left him in charge of the store when he went out to lunch. The store handled a wide variety of gift items as well as books, and Leseur noticed that gold pens, watch chains and other jewelry disappeared while he was gone.

"One day I spied from the Gilsey House," he recalled. "There was Williamson, stuffing small items into his pockets. I was furious, I can tell you. I ran back to my store and confronted him. But do you know, he made good the loss and seemed so sincerely repentant that I couldn't help but forgive him."

(All of these investigations and news accounts, it must be borne in mind, occurred after Williamson's arrest in Baltimore and return to New York. The press tried faithfully to compile a complete and accurate history, but Williamson himself was often surprisingly wordless about great chunks of his career and the information the papers got was at times fragmentary in the extreme.)

It was shortly after this that Williamson was dismissed as a teacher at Trinity Chapel, a scandal that sent him packing off to St. Louis again. The papers endeavored to pick up his trail in St. Louis, the Pittsburgh *Gazette* being the only one to have any appreciable success, saying in a dispatch datelined from the Missouri city that Williamson "is a character well known in St. Louis." This was the only newspaper account to suggest that he ever used liquor more than a vestryman should: "He was here connected with the Pullman Palace Car Company in 1872, and, possessing a good address, managed to secure a good position in society. He became connected with Christ Church, Episcopal, and founded a mission school, though, at the same time, in the habit of giving lively parties in his rooms on Saturday nights, the conviviality of which generally extended late into Sunday morning. He finally became engaged in a quarrel with another man in his own circle, and there was at the time a good deal of gossip over a projected duel. It appears that from here Williamson went to London." The New York *Times*, the only other paper to give even a driblet of information about this St. Louis interlude, said vaguely that he took punishment in "a cowhiding scrape in which he stood at the lash-end of a whip, [which] suddenly caused his departure to other climates, and saved a wealthy girl from falling a victim to his polished villainy."

The *Times* did not define his polished villainy, evidently feeling that in 1880 anyone understood what the term meant when used to describe a gentleman's relations with a lady. The fact that the *Gazette* mentions a projected duel but no cowhiding, while the *Times* tells of a cowhiding but no duel, makes the conscientious historian throw up his hands in dismay. So also does the casual tossing off of the statement that he "founded a mission school," as if this were a common achievement of men who visited St. Louis.

In any case it seems safe to say that he encountered trouble of some sort there. Yet his intrepid spirit was undaunted. En route to Europe once more, he stopped off at the Fifth Avenue Hotel in New York for a time, again showing his preference for the best hotels. So far he had always paid his hotel bills, although he was less careful about smaller obligations that could be skipped without loud outcry. At Pillsbury's stationery store he ordered five hundred engraved cards announcing, in French, the marriage of Colonel E. E. Fairfax

Williamson to "Adelaide de la Roche Aymon, Comtesse de Maro-lies," to take place at Hyères *"Lundi, le vingt-et-un de septembre, 1872, à midi."* Neglecting to pay Pillsbury's, the colonel set sail and later mailed the cards from Paris. He followed them with another card, this one in English, saying that acceptance or regrets could be sent him after August tenth "in care of Bowles Brothers and Company, bankers, Rue de la Paix, Paris." All this had caused considerable excitement among hundreds of acquaintances in St. Louis, Chicago, Baltimore, Pittsburgh, New York, and presumably among those in Europe. Williamson was such a likable man that many of his American friends had written in care of Bowles Brothers regretting their inability to cross the ocean for the wedding, some of them sending gifts instead.

(But Hyères had never experienced this glad occasion. A Baltimore couple friendly with Williamson happened to be on the Riviera at the time. They hastened over to Hyères, bearing gifts, and canvassed the churches. It soon became clear not only that no wedding had been arranged for but that no one there had so much as heard of either Williamson or the Countess Adelaide. It was now discovered that the countess did not exist.)

Students of Hookiana noted that so far as was known, this hoax was Williamson's first uncertain, faltering variation on the Berners Street theme. It was clear that in addition to a sharp sense of the comic he had a painfully sensitive spirit and the kind of compulsion to flatter his own ego that often whets the creative impulse. Wounded by a succession of reverses in America, he had felt forced to rebuild himself in the public estimation (and therefore his own) by staging this fake marriage to a countess. Though successful enough in deception, and embodying an interesting international involvement, it was otherwise a weak effort artistically. Beginning with the heavy and fraudulent use of the mails which was the hallmark of both Hook's and Williamson's work, it fell down, to use chess parlance, in the middle and end games. It lacked the important element of sadistic excitement, since it imposed no real hardship on those receiving the cards—even those who sent wedding gifts. It was devoid of secrecy, suspense and risk, for Williamson was the known "bridegroom" and even if caught he could hardly be arrested, sued or flogged for such a comparatively innocuous trick. Above all, it was wanting in the essential ingredient, the central victim who suffered ludicrous inconvenience (as with Mrs. Tottenham) or the small group of cleverly related victims (as with Dr. Dix et al.). Still, one must walk before he can run. It was as interesting to find this early Williamson effort as for a Dickens scholar to trace that novelist's first newspaper stories.

CHAPTER XIV

EXPANDING TALENTS

In October, 1872, three weeks after his Riviera idyll, Williamson arrived *solus* at the fashionable Hotel Metropole in Geneva. If he had always taken a quiet satisfaction in his Fairfax ancestry, he evidently now decided that the great name should take precedence over his own diffidence, for he registered as Colonel E. Fairfax Williamson de Fairfax. He produced letters of introduction from his old friend, Bishop Whitehouse, from "Major, the Hon. Fairfax Stuart Fairfax" and other dignitaries in America and Europe (all now believed to have been forged). He ran out of money very quickly, but his charm and testimonials won him unlimited credit that enabled him to continue living in one of the Metropole's best suites, to cut a dash in the Quartier Saint-Gervais and to indulge his pleasant penchant for gift-giving.

Geneva was a center for the manufacture of music boxes—a craft begun as a sideline by local watchmakers but soon thriving on its own—and it was here that he amassed the collection that made him famous. He showed little interest in those that had no disguise—that is, music boxes which were simply music boxes. What caught his fancy were musical teapots, snuff boxes, Toby jugs, walking sticks, chamber pots and clocks. He called in artisans to do custom work for him such as installing a music box that automatically greeted guests with "Welcome, Sweet Friend" the moment the door was opened, and others in his escritoire and other pieces of furniture. One could not sit down in his apartment without setting atinkle "Frühlingsstimmen," "Frère Jacques" or the Minuet from Mozart's "Serenade in E Flat." "The sofa," said one account, "yielded lugubrious German strains, while the footstools, when pressed upon, gave out lively French melodies." He had a decanter that played drinking songs when wine was poured, musical beer mugs and a *port-monnaie* that burst into "Die Wacht am Rhein" when opened. A hotel servant was charged with the duty of winding the music boxes several times daily, as well as a dozen-odd mechanical singing birds perched about the place. His favorite of all hymns, "The King of Love My Shepherd Is," was not available in any music-box form, nor was "Dixie," the song that stirred his Fairfax blood. He supplied the music and tried to persuade a craftsman to make a cylinder of each for him alone. By this time, however, he owed a great deal for previous work and was unable to get more done without something stronger than promises.

As always, he was a faithful Episcopal communicant, strictly High Church. He became a favorite in the American colony despite a certain mystery that clung to him, and even some of the English and French sojourners there (he spoke excellent French) had to agree that Monsieur le Colonel was engaging. This was a time when not a few American robber barons lost esteem for themselves and their country because of their arrogance in buying only the most expensive objects, be they paintings or pewter, chiefly to show their wealth. Williamson de Fairfax's music-box fancy was by contrast unpretentious and refreshing, as was his habit of giving gold pens or pencils to acquaintances. Although he varied these with other gifts, he often said truly that no present could give him so much selfish pleasure because the recipient was reminded and expected to write him. No one at the time, of course, could possibly foresee what novel directions his preoccupation with pens and writing would ultimately lead him in.

He liked to walk each morning in the Place des Alpes singing "Gloria in Excelsis Deo" to himself in his reedy tenor, unmindful of the stares of passersby. He visited the Château de Lancy just outside of town where a German professor had established a preparatory school which numbered among its students scions of the Colgate and McVickars families of New York and the son of George Francis Train. Sure enough, he presented the teachers and the American pupils with gold pens, and he returned weekly to join in the religious services and discuss educational problems. He spent several hours each day writing letters. His notepaper bore the Fairfax crest in red, blue and gold, the same crest being embroidered on his linen and stamped in every one of his considerable number of books. He left carelessly around his lodgings, where they were certain to be seen, calling cards from noted personages who evidently had stopped in, and letters from various Fairfaxes and members of the European nobility. On several occasions he asked guests to mail his letters to the deposed Empress Eugénie, who he said was one of his dearest friends.

But like gifted people in whatever field, he could continue for only a limited time in work that utilized no more than a part of his abilities. Periodically he needed a challenge drawing on his deeper talents. A practical consideration also had to be faced: whatever source it was that ordinarily supplied him with money had gone as dry as Dr. Dix's sermons. His creditors were pressing him. It seems that by spring, too, the example of Hook began to kindle his spirit again. It was an especially romantic season in lovely Geneva, with its memories of Rousseau and Byron, its band music on the Promenade du Lac, and with young men from the university taking town girls for boat rides on the lake.

The colonel let a few of his friends know confidentially that he would soon be married. He resolutely refused to name the lady, saying that she would be known in good time and that she was, of course, listed in the *Almanach de Gotha*. This news, being confidential, spread and caused great curiosity—just one example of his gift for publicity. He sent out a thousand invitations to friends and acquaintances, and to friends and acquaintances of friends and acquaintances. He never bothered to follow strict formality in such matters. Unlike the announcements of his marriage to the Comtesse de Marolies, these invitations were handwritten, taking him considerable time. A throng of guests appeared, formally dressed, at the Church of St.-Pierre on the day named. They got word that there had been some mistake, no wedding being scheduled. They milled around *la cour St.-Pierre* in doubt or anger. (The New York *Herald*, which printed the most complete account of the incident eight years later, in 1880, broke one of journalism's sternest canons by failing to get the name of the mythical bride-to-be.) As for Williamson, he stationed himself at a window across the street where the view was unobstructed. "There were hundreds of my friends and their friends waiting for the ceremony to begin," he told the *Herald*, "but it did not begin. There was nobody to begin with. This was one of a great many of what I may call my practical jokes. They were harmless."

Still, the incident caused annoyance. This, along with his debts, made a quick departure advisable. He vanished from Geneva owing something over $5,000 to the hotel, the gift shops, the music-box makers and several friends.

(As far as could be discovered, this was the first time he had run out on debts of such size, and he later defended his intentions if not his fiscal practices: "Yes, I got in debt. That was my misfortune, and one that might happen to any man. I did not intend to cheat anyone, and tried to pay all [my obligations]. I did afterward give notes to some persons, and paid some of them—as many as I could." At least one of the music-box men must have been paid, for Williamson received a part of the collection he had been forced to leave behind him. Though the investigators could only guess, they felt it likely that his wealthy family had made good his debts on many occasions, particularly in the United States, where nonpayment might stir up an embarrassing scandal. It was thought probable that he had worn out their patience in this respect and that in the Geneva affair they had let the wastrel solve his own problems. These, however, were only theories and would ultimately be disproven, to leave some aspects of Williamson's career more puzzling than ever.)

His next stop was London where, for a man harassed by debt, he lived very comfortably, as usual without working. Again he became a devout Anglican, a strenuous Fairfax and a loyal Confederate. He introduced himself as a former lieutenant colonel in "the Virginia Division of the Confederate Army," and sent letters to his friends notifying them of his legal right to the Fairfax name. No matter what trouble he got into under that great name in one city, he so revered it that he not only used it but advertised it in the next— this despite the sizable English colony in Geneva and the chance that news of his exploits (and debts) there would reach London. Although in his whole career he left not only Geneva but also Baltimore, London, New York and St. Louis (and who knew how many other cities?) under some sort of cloud, he had always popped up in the next city to blow his horn as a Fairfax of the Williamson branch. The use of the name might easily have caused him embarrassment or arrest, but it seemed never to have done so. He almost seemed to *dare* the police to suspect him. This Fairfax-Williamson loyalty was one of many aspects of his behavior that puzzled Captain Byrnes, for it removed him from the class of the common swindler who has a new name in every town. Byrnes, who knew hundreds of clever bunco artists, was unable to place Williamson in that or any other category of crime. He seemed unclassifiable. But whatever one wanted to call him, Byrnes felt, one quality that made him great was his absolute indomitable fearlessness in facing the world, name and all, as if he were an honest man. Rumors from Pittsburgh, however, suggested that Williamson's own relatives, uneasy about his escapades, would have been happier had he used another name entirely. To his many New York admirers of 1880, on the other hand, his stubborn retention of his name was an endearing quality proving his courage and consistency even in falsehood.

He lodged briefly with the Rosenbaums in Bloomsbury and became friendly with at least a few prominent Anglicans, including Richard Shaw, Member of Parliament for Burnley, and a wealthy broker named Gordon Thomas. He continued his compulsive letter-writing to friends in Europe and America, telling some of them that he was betrothed to a London heiress. After his quarrel with Rosenbaum he moved to the Hotel Langham, then broadcast the letters that brought hundreds of callers to the Rosenbaum home.

To the more scholarly Hook-ites, the searchers for the signs of growth in genius, the Rosenbaum case had a special interest. It was the first time, as far as was yet known, that Williamson had followed the classic Hook principles and produced a work of genuine, if limited, merit. His Geneva production, lightly amusing though it was, had the same shortcomings as his Hyères hoax and really derived most of its charm from its music-box accompaniment. The Rosenbaum affair had the traditional essentials, including the central victim, the secrecy, suspense and risk. It took Williamson out of the eddies and put him squarely in the mainstream of jokesmanship. That the risk was all too real was proved by his detection after being in London less than three months and his conviction in August,

1873—a misfortune that ended his betrothal to the heiress, who, it could be safely assumed, had never existed.

It is doubtful that even his admirers—those who understood him best—realized what an ordeal that year in Pentonville Prison was for the fancier of *belles-lettres*, chamber music and *petits fours*. As luck would have it, the ferocious, lantern-jawed Sir Edmund Du Cane, eight years in office as Chairman of Prison Commissioners, had now had sufficient time to implement his conviction that if gaols were made repellent enough, criminals would reform out of sheer self-preservation. He demonstrated that prisons, innately unpleasant, could be made much more so when real intelligence and effort were applied to the problem. To the sociable and gregarious Williamson the rule of silence alone was a refinement of torture. Pentonville was a bleak horror that would have turned almost anyone else away from risking such punishment again. As it was, it turned him only against England, which he never visited thereafter and never spoke of without some bitterness.

When he was released in 1874, he hurried to Paris and entered another of those underground periods—this one of about a year—during which his activities could not be traced and which he declined to discuss. In 1875 he returned to New York where, even before he had time to establish strong churchly connections, he was arrested on the charge of the messenger boy. Again, although he was now technically a fugitive from justice after he jumped his bail, he emerged in Pittsburgh as Eugene Edward Fairfax Williamson, just as he had been in New York. This loyalty, however, seemed to have been more for the name than for his own closest relatives—or perhaps their own loyalty for *him* had flagged. In any case, he avoided them, set up his bachelor's quarters on the East Side and joined St. Andrew's. For a few months he worked as a bookkeeper for the National Tube Company—a job probably obtained through his brother, the vice president. It seemed to have been his only regularly salaried position since his brief Pullman berth in St. Louis. Obviously this drudgery soon would have crushed the élan of the worshiper of Hook. He resigned, although his work was satisfactory, and resumed his proper station as a gentleman of leisure, devoting his time to church work, children, social gatherings, mysterious trips out of town and the encouragement of worthy causes.

Never below the top in his list of worthy causes was the delicate promotion of self that had characterized him since boyhood. He noted that the popularity of baseball had soared. As a Pittsburgh dispatch to the New York *Sun* reported, "He uniformed and equipped a base ball club, and it took the name of the Eugene Fairfax Base Ball Club." The name "Williamson" had entirely too many letters to sew on a baseball shirt, and besides it was really the Fairfax connection that he wanted to stress. His team played others in the area, and although he was never able to understand the complexities of the game he was usually there to cheer his men. He did better than that. Lover of music that he was, he bought band instruments for a group of musicians who became known as the Eugene Fairfax Band and who played at all games.

Here again there was subtle mention of the peculiarity that was never brought out into the open: "The objects of his generosity in two instances were boys—one the son of a leading financier of the city, the other of a contractor. To the first he offered a rare diamond pin, but the mother of the lad would not allow him to accept it. In the other instance, the gift proposed was a gold watch and chain, and was also returned." But it was clear that he had observed reasonable decorum since he had spent most of the last five years in Pittsburgh, with his reputation actually improving. He was obviously fond of all children, for he had taken large groups of Episcopalian boys and girls to museums, concerts and the circus, paying for everything including peanuts and lollipops.

Just as a diversion (and to keep his own name in print) he

contributed poetry and bouncy society items to the local paper. Gregarious, witty, fluent, he liked to dash off verses dedicated to his lady friends, of whom he had a few, whether out of real interest or for social convenience. To them and to friends in general he gave away many copies of his books, always inscribed with graceful sentiments. He was a confirmed bestower of flowers. Also, the *Herald* noted, "... on several occasions he gave some married ladies packets of seeds of rare plants which had been sent to him from Europe, and the queer part of it was that the flowers when they came to perfection proved to be hollyhocks, daisies or other common varieties."

CHAPTER XV

THE THORNY PATH I TREAD

That was the extent of the dossier on Williamson compiled by the police and the newspapers. One might have thought that by now he would have been stripped of the glamour that seems as essential to a public figure as to a reigning belle, and that the exotic blossom of the Fairfaxes would be dismissed as a hollyhock himself. Not so. Even the revelation that he had been a petty purloiner of fountain pens could not undo the fascination of his activities in Geneva, London, New York and Pittsburgh. In a sense it added to the preposterousness of the riddle he presented—the spectacle of a man who steals pens but gives away tubas, gold watches and diamond pins. He was a subject of animated discussion at cultivated social gatherings. Those who pondered most keenly about him (it was said they had a glint of envy in their eyes) were apt to be honest, substantial burghers who outwardly deplored his behavior. He had freed himself entirely from the harness of puritanism so universally worn and so choking, and trotted off unrestrained. His eccentricities, when analyzed, seemed to consist largely of doing what he pleased, never deterred by considerations of duty, expense or honesty. With few exceptions he seemed to have had a whale of a good time. It is not impossible that he was secretly honored not only for furnishing amusement but also for his oblique attack on smugness. If he did not subject society to explicit Voltairean criticism, he did nevertheless illuminate some of its absurdities.

His admirers noted that there were great lacunae in the dossier. Nothing was known of his career from 1857 to 1863, from 1864 to 1868, for a whole year in 1874–75, and several other periods of many months before and since then. For example, he had been based in Pittsburgh since 1875, but he had occasionally disappeared for long periods when he might have been in New York or elsewhere. He had done so many unusual things during those intervals when his activities could be followed that it was felt almost certain that there would be accomplishments of equal interest during the others. This feeling was heightened by Williamson's polite refusal to fill in the lacunae. He did once say that he had traveled in England, France, the Low Countries, Germany, Italy, Switzerland and Spain. Since his activities were known (in small part) only in England, France and Switzerland, one can imagine the pitch of the curiosity about his enterprises elsewhere.

Who could tell in how many other instances he had emulated or excelled Theodore Hook—in how many cities? Reporters kept urging him to disclose the rest of his career—in effect, to furnish his autobiography. He declined, probably fearing heavier punishment. Indeed he would have said nothing about the Hyères, Geneva and London performances had they not become known through other channels. Thus he was in the position of a newly discovered painter who has created several known and charming canvases and who insists on keeping dozens of others locked in his garret, unseen.

All along, since his arrest, Williamson had seemed a man in a hurry. He had been anxious to return to New York so that he could make his personal appeal to Dr. Dix. He had been greatly downcast by the failure of his interview with the rector. He was hoping for a second opportunity to present his case to him. Since everything he said was quoted in the papers, he was careful (after some minor early errors) to speak with the dignity and remorse which he felt might soften Dr. Dix. Meanwhile, he gnawed his nails in impatience. Had one been of a suspicious nature, one might have thought Williamson anxious to dispose quickly of the current charges against him before more could be brought.

Captain Byrnes had just such a suspicious nature. He was in charge of the criminal investigation, the Post Office men's work having been in effect finished with the capture. He had his men make a careful search of Williamson's baggage. They found (in addition to signed photographs of Sir William and Lady Fairfax of the English branch) many blank checks in the name of the Pittsburgh Forge & Iron Company and other firms of that city. Lo, the suspicions were justified. Williamson, in detectives' argot, was a paperhanger. Under the name of Edward P. Adams and other aliases, he had swindled a dozen jewelry firms, including the J. E. Caldwell Company of Philadelphia, and Tiffany's and Howard & Company of New York, through forged checks. From each of these companies he had bought gold pens, signet rings, diamond pins, watches, cufflinks and other jewelry, paying for them with fraudulent checks never exceeding $100. The gold watch he had offered Colonel Bliss proved to be one of the items acquired in this way—price, $67.50 at Howard's. Yet the search of his luggage and rooms indicated that this was the only one he had kept for himself. Evidently he had given all the others away.

When the news was taken to Williamson in his cell, he blanched. He pondered gloomily for several minutes before he seemed to reach the conclusion that there was nothing to do but put the best face on it he could.

"These things did not do me any good," he said, "for I gave them away to friends just as freely as George William Childs, of Philadelphia, gives away cups and saucers. You know, perhaps, that to every lady who calls upon him he gives away a cup and saucer on which is inscribed his portrait and autograph. Odd fancy, is it not?... This cup and saucer gift is one of his fancies, and mine was a similar one.... I don't know why it is, but I have an uncontrollable bent that way."

Childs, the wealthy publisher of the *Public Ledger*, agreed about the similarity when he was told of Williamson's remark. "But there is one important difference," he pointed out. "I don't steal my cups and saucers."

Still, Williamson's followers (who now evidently were spread over many of the Eastern states in view of the coverage by the New York, Philadelphia, Pittsburgh, Baltimore and Richmond papers) felt that his recovery was admirable under the circumstances. How many forgers could have put such an innocent and charming construction on their handiwork?—especially since it was true that he had invariably given the jewelry away. His life continued to unfold in driblets as the police and the newspapers looked diligently for further installments. Inquiries in Baltimore disclosed that Eugene Edward Fairfax Williamson was listed in the current city directory there—but at an address on Charles Street that was discovered not to exist. Although this address seemed the perfect one for a man who had embarked on so many fictitious adventures, fought so many imaginary battles, assumed so many legendary titles and married so many non-existent women, it aroused even heavier police suspicions. His frequent trips away from Pittsburgh were recalled and it was reasoned that he must have carried on extensive criminal operations in Maryland. Yet none of his rubber checks were found bouncing around Baltimore, nor were there any swindled jewelers or signs of other illegality. Williamson himself said blandly that the fictitious address was a mystery to him and must certainly have been a misprint—a likely story. No one could divine the reason for it except to surmise that the reason could hardly have been an innocent one, and this little puzzle in Baltimore served only to thicken the mystery that already surrounded him like a halo of pea soup. He was obviously growing ever more anxious, for he tried to repair his public image with a statement admitting some error but stressing his fundamental generosity.

"I have done foolish things," he said in part, "but never in any spirit of malice, and in fact I cannot even explain what prompted me to do these things. At times I seem unable to resist my impulses, although you must concede that many of them are not really bad. It's like those musical instruments I gave to my friends. When I come to think of it, I have given away all the money I ever had. In Pittsburgh I was known as the children's friend and used to take them out on picnics and excursions. They will tell you I'm not a bad fellow at heart."

Now a new actor strode indignantly to center stage—Major M. P. Haverty, a New York publisher of Catholic books. "Williamson is the greatest plagiarist unhung," he said. The four religious dramas claimed by the prisoner, he said, were actually the work of a nun, Sister Ambrosine of Yonkers, and so were the two sacred poems. Haverty had published this entire complement of Sister Ambrosine's work in one large volume in 1873. He had the volume and Sister Ambrosine's statement to prove it. Williamson had first lifted *The Sisters of Alhambra*, republishing it as a small book of pocket size after making minor changes where he felt the wording could be improved.* This had been so successful in Pittsburgh and elsewhere that he had gone ahead with the others in succession. Major Haverty brought suit against Stevenson & Foster for infringement of copyright—a

---

*Miriam, "by E. Fairfax Williamson," is still available [as of 1968] at the New York Public Library. Sister Ambrosine's works are not to be found there.

further vexation to Stevenson & Foster, who had not yet been paid for the printing by Williamson although he always paid his pew rent at St. Andrew's on the dot.

The New York *Tribune* suffered considerable derision from its contemporaries because of its praise for Williamson's "faultless melody," "vivid imagination," and its assurance of his "undoubted place in the front rank of our new poets." A *Tribune* editorial said huffily, "Sometimes we come across a man who is so wholly and completely false that he can only be regarded as a psychological curiosity; and Mr. Eugene Fairfax Williamson seems to be one of this class.... It does not seem to have been possible for Williamson to do anything squarely and honestly.... Trickery became as natural to him as breathing."

It appeared that for Williamson, the discovery of his plagiarism was the cruelest blow of all. It injured the intellectual standing he had taken such pride in, as well as his pretensions to walk in the footsteps of Hook. Through the dozens of reporters who visited him, he knew that he had a public following and that he had disappointed it. To steal pens and pencils, to forge checks, to draw the long bow—these things could be overlooked so long as he was "in the front rank of our new poets." Now that laurel had been taken from him. But even yet there were a few newsmen who felt that his literary reputation was not entirely spurious. The changes he had made in Sister Ambrosine's work were all for the better. The man had an ear for rhetoric, no doubt of it. They had talked with him enough to know that he could quote Byron or Wordsworth by the stanza, and that he could also dash off rhymes that appeared to be (or were they?) his own. After all, his Dix letters were themselves proof of his facility, as were his newspaper writings. In Pittsburgh he had given a copy of *Little Golden Hair* to four young sisters and had inscribed it to "four of the dear young folks, Clara, Louise, Nannie, Agnes," under which he wrote:

Sweet maidens, in the rosy light
Of youthful beauty dwelling,
I send you now this simple play
From Love's deep fountain swelling.

It has no grace nor charm of verse
But is an earnest feeling:
A deepened tone from out my heart
Like from sweet music stealing.

If in the thorny path I tread
My feet have missed the flowers,
I have four buds of beauty left
With which to grace my bowers.

And should I dwell 'neath cloudy skies
With not a star to cheer me
I'll think upon your lovely eyes
And feel that stars are near me.

This was not bad stuff, his defenders argued, and it seemed so aptly aimed at the four sisters that it could hardly be plagiarized (or could it?).* There was a rush for the poetry books and anthologies, but the poem could not be found. A group of die-hard cynics took the opposite view. Nothing could be more damaging to The Lord or more slanderous, they argued, than to say that this poem or anything else he wrote was original, or that anything he did was honest, since his whole reputation was founded on complete, utter, unmitigated fraud.

Questioned about his literary work, Williamson said regretfully that he could not discuss it. He had taken a momentous step. He had

---

*Also plagiarized, alas, from Essie B. Cheeseborough's poem "Nina and Maria" (c. 1855). —P. C.

retained the lawyers Howe & Hummel, whose invariable advice to clients was, "Don't talk—we'll do that for you."

To engage the notorious Howe & Hummel was to tell the world that one no longer cared about his social standing; one merely wanted to beat the rap. This as much as anything else showed the desperation to which Williamson, the lover of society, had been driven by the scandal which had ruined him anyway, and by his loathing for the Tombs and the looming threat of Sing Sing ahead. Howe & Hummel represented all the big-time crooks in the city, and those of the small-timers who could pay their extortionate fees. They not only represented criminals but were eminent criminals themselves, often cutting the pie with malefic accomplices. Once, when seventy-four brothel madams were arrested in a periodic cleanup, each of the seventy-four unhesitatingly selected Howe & Hummel as their attorneys. The two were expert at manufacturing evidence, bribing and intimidating witnesses and jurors, slipping thousand-dollar bills to complaisant judges and in joining with lovely stage girls in the blackmailing of wealthy men-about-town. William F. Howe, the senior partner, was a big, red-faced mountebank who had served time in an English prison—a fact that would give him exceptional rapport with Williamson. He wore racetrack plaids and a diamond of at least three carats on every finger of both hands. Known as The Weeper, he was famous for his ability to work even unbribed juries up to a pitch of emotion which he could gauge with unerring instinct, and then, just at the right moment, fall to his knees and break them up with a flood of crocodile tears. The ease with which he could produce instant tears was the envy of all other criminal lawyers. His junior colleague, Abraham H. Hummel, was almost a midget, a shade smaller than Williamson—the fox, the fixer, the creator of spurious evidence. The fact that Howe & Hummel consented to take Williamson's case proved that they knew of his wealthy family, since he had less than $75 on him when he was arrested.

Although the evidence against him was perfectly clear, this was no proof that Howe & Hummel could not get him a negligible sentence or free him entirely. Again and again they had performed such miracles as liberating "Mother" Mandelbaum, the city's wealthiest crime organizer and fence, springing the scandalous Victoria Woodhull from prison and saving the neck of Ned Stokes, who had murdered Jim Fisk in broad daylight. Williamson indeed seemed their ideal client—small, cultivated, good-looking, appealing, just the sort over whom Howe could blubber most effectively.

Looking at it from the point of view of the district attorney, the dossier on Williamson, incomplete though it was, seemed sufficient to establish a consistent pattern of fraudulent behavior. Gripped by a helpless passion for self-glorification, he had trotted the globe as a living fiction, assuming titles, distributing largess, surrounding himself with legend, perfecting a British accent, embracing fashionable Episcopacy, mingling with the *beau monde*, honoring the great Theodore Hook, moving from place to place when his impostures or his bills caught up with him. The most baffling mystery yet remaining was the question of how he had paid his way.

His forgeries, as far as they were known, were petty when compared with his expenditures. Much of the time for the past twenty years the carpet knight with no known income had lived on a scale approaching wealth. If it was true that he had occasionally fled his debts, he had more often paid them in full. One did not live at the Windsor in New York or the Langham in London on a clerkship, nor did one give away diamond pins and gold watches, or outfit baseball teams and brass bands. The assumption that his family had subsidized him turned out to be mistaken. His brother, sister and mother all denied having given him so much as a dollar for many years. He had been on his own ever since the war, they said. They might hear from him once a year or so—charming notes that told nothing about how he made his living. Although he had been kind to them, their bourgeois standards had bored him; the skylark had to fly as he willed. They had not even known until now of his imprisonment in England seven years earlier. His brother Alfred had got him the short-lived job at the National Tube Company but had scarcely seen him even then, for they worked far apart. The family were agreed that Eugene was mentally irresponsible, the mother saying that he had long been "eccentric, and even demented," and Alfred saying more vigorously, "He has several times been quite out of his mind." As for his good friend and pastor, Dr. Reese Alsop, he agreed that Williamson was an odd one but that he had some admirable qualities—so much so that Alsop was writing Dr. Dix in his behalf.

Still—where did he get all that money? "He certainly had no business so lucrative as to support him as he had lived much of the time," said the *Tribune*, suggesting that he must be concealing enormous swindles. His income became the subject of almost as much speculation as that of the late Boss Tweed. Some argued that it was not necessarily huge, since he alternated his splurges with niggling economies—as witness his stealing of pens to use as gifts and his use of penny postcards in the Dix case. Others were sure he was an international embezzler, a blackmailer of wealthy women or a lucky plunger in the market. Williamson, with his artist's soul all but bared, refused to doff this last little drape. He would not disclose the source of his wealth. The answer given by this man who had had virtually no known honest income for years was in his best vein of the absurd: "I *did* save my money at times for a bit of a fête."

CHAPTER XVI

THE DUKE OF SING SING

On Easter Sunday, March twenty-eighth, Dr. Dix must indeed have experienced a sense of spiritual resurrection as he conducted the services at old Trinity before an altar trimmed with wreaths and crosses and a reredos decorated with thousands of lilies. The criticisms of Low Churchmen, the insults of atheists, the jealousy of Trinity's wealth, the wild claims of the Bogardus "descendants" were all part of his duty, accepted as routine, having at least the virtue of uniting his parish in solidarity behind him. Not so the mad whim of Gentleman Joe, which had unnerved him with the menace of the unknown, distracted his wife and spread dark suspicions in all his seven churches.

The joy of Easter! "The processional hymn of the white-robed choir began," said the *Sun*, "faint and low, in a closed room behind the chancel. The chimes ceased ringing. Suddenly, at an expression of joy in the hymn, a door opened, and the church was flooded with the chorus of exultant voices." Then the rituals hallowed by the centuries—the Kyrie eleison, the Gloria, the Nicene Creed, the Sanctus and the Agnus Dei. Dr. Dix, straight as a ramrod in his glistening robe, preached from a text in the nineteenth chapter of St. John. "This morning," he said, "you come here with light and happy souls to hear the chimes and the anthem. The altar beams out and flowers unfold their bright leaves. And you are not alone in this, and up to heaven there goes this day how vast a host of praises and trusts!... The return of Christ, this most certain truth... is the one great fact of history, the hinge on which the world revolves."

The rector's own world had been unhinged for more than five weeks. One could hardly blame him if a small fraction of the lightness and happiness in his own soul came less from contemplation of the risen Christ than from relief over the imprisoned Gentleman Joe. The splendor of the Easter service was almost matched by the color and luxury of new gowns with a suggestion of the soon-to-be-modish bustle, new hats with brilliant feathers, new men's tailoring beyond the chancel. As always on this great day, the streets outside were choked with broughams and landaus tended by cocked-hatted coachmen who gossiped as they waited their masters' return from worship. At the Tombs a mile to the north, Eugene Fairfax Williamson's sybaritic soul was offended as he sat among pickpockets, pimps and other felons and heard a service read by a threadbare pastor named Wiggins from the Pearl Street Mission.

From the start, Williamson had known that his fate lay largely in the hands of Dr. Dix, who had the option of using his powerful prestige in the little man's favor. The latter, worldling that he was, understood that this was so despite the fact that his crimes were what they were whatever the rector thought of them, that the law should judge them without regard for the victim's opinion and that it was another facet of improper influence to give the rector any authority in the matter. Dr. Dix did not seem to realize this. He lived in a world that took upper-class hegemony for granted.

But Williamson, with his sharp sense of realism, should have seen that his hope for clemency was a vain one. Even the spirit of Easter could hardly move Dr. Dix from his conviction that Gentleman Joe was too unstable mentally and morally to be allowed to remain at large. Dr. Alsop's letter, whatever it said, did not move him, nor did the fact that the rascal had been kind to such as Clara, Louise, Nannie and Agnes. Certainly the rector did not permit himself the kind of imaginative flight that would have persuaded him that he and Williamson were, after all, both sincere worshipers, though at different shrines, Williamson giving his devotion to Theodore Hook. Dr. Dix was a good man, but a good man of the eighteenth rather than the nineteenth century. Hell was real to him. One feels that he was certain that Williamson was speeding toward hell and indeed that he *belonged* there.

As Colonel Bliss put it, "Dr. Dix considers Williamson's case entirely out of his hands now, and he certainly will not interfere to save the man from punishment."

From the respectable portion of the Williamson family in Pittsburgh came a sharp message that seemed to snatch away the prisoner's last chance to wriggle free. The family had heard about Howe & Hummel. They preferred not to be associated with such counsel. They dismissed Howe & Hummel and retained Algernon S. Sullivan of the eminently respectable New York firm of Sullivan & Cromwell. Although Sullivan was rated an excellent lawyer in such matters as wills and contracts, the fraudulent liberation of criminals was outside his domain. Never in his career at the bar had he squeezed out a counterfeit tear, and it appeared that nothing but Howe's weeping (and Hummel's bribes) could rescue Williamson now.

Sullivan made cautious double-talk about his client, saying, "I am assured by the most respected authorities that if not actually insane he is subject to such a degree of mental aberration and irregularity as amounts to a demented state." Sullivan obviously was trying to palliate Williamson's crimes on the score of instability without condemning him to the madhouse on Blackwell's Island, a fearsome place in 1880. Alfred Williamson made a quick trip to New York to see Sullivan and also to see his errant younger brother, who seemed deeply affected by the visit. "I knew my family would not abandon me," he said. His only other visitors were the ubiquitous reporters and "Miss Davis and Miss Griffin of the Tombs Mission Society, who spoke a few words of sympathy to him." Docile and resigned, he said, "I don't know what I shall plead. I will plead however counsel says."

So the mills of justice began one of their more coarsely ground violations of truth as Williamson was indicted on charges of forgery and attempted extortion. To be sure, he had forged hundreds of letters and many checks, but the evidence seemed clear to those who could read it that the extortion charge was false. All along the investigators had missed the point in their estimate of his motive in writing the cards involving Dr. Dix. They had looked hard for a grudge against the rector. Unable to find one, they had fallen back on the extortion theory. In one sense the error was a mere technicality, for it probably made no difference in Williamson's ultimate fate. But it was of first importance in its illustration of the quagmire of misunderstanding the law could sink into when confronted by the esoteric. Blackstone and the muses could not communicate. They spoke different languages.

Hundreds of armchair experts in the Eastern seaboard area— close students of Hook and Williamson—could have corrected the error. If Williamson had really intended extortion, why had he made no effort to consummate it? Does an extortionist seriously seeking money in New York pull up stakes and head for Chicago via Baltimore? Did not Williamson's many letters to Buckley, Boden, the newspapers and others further discredit the idea that he sought profit? Had not his Hyères and Geneva performances clearly been done with no grudge and no thought of gain? Did not his Rosen-baum production in London, where there *was* a grudge and also a demand for money that was unpursued and came to nothing, show clearly that the demand was simply a part of the hoax?

The New York authorities could not seem to realize that for him an artistic motive was enough. Even yet they did not grasp the fact that they and their whole city had been manipulated in a vast achievement of dramaturgy—that this whole enterprise of William-son's was the result of a theatrical concept never before approached in ambition, scope and daring. He had appointed himself writer, producer, director and stage manager for a drama encompassing the metropolis, using its streets, churches and buildings as his stage, its newspapers as his publicity organs, and a huge complement of citi-zens, manufacturers, business and professional men, the police and public officials as his players. As casting director he had picked the famous, dignified, severe and sensation-hating Dr. Dix to be a victim simply because he would be perfect in the role, the man best en-dowed to react entertainingly and with maximum publicity. Various scenes in his extravaganza were laid in Twenty-fifth Street, Trinity Church, Trinity Chapel, Buckley's saloon, the newspaper offices and other places. And as producer, Williamson had proudly entered—this time as a spectator, a part of the audience—the real-life the-ater he alone and unaided had devised. He had paraded Twenty-fifth Street to watch the comedy which he had framed for the living world and whose critics gave him front-page space in every newspaper in town. It made him feel like a god—and why not?—to see and read of thousands of people in his cast enacting, all unknowing, the roles he had created for them, with literally millions watching in the news-papers a drama so suspenseful that it continued for weeks.

Let Aristophanes tumble from his pedestal. Let Shakespeare crash with him. No one in the world but Williamson (with the possible ex-ception of Hook) had thought in terms of such theatrical magnitude.

An unidentified relative stressed this theatrical instinct in a letter to Attorney Sullivan, saying that Williamson had always had "a powerful yearning to create sensations and gain notoriety." Another relative, probably Alfred Williamson, wrote the lawyer about the prisoner's instability: "He is... a man of super-nervous, excitable temperament, uncontrollable passion when excited, at the same time of very sensitive feelings. While at home he would at times exhibit the most intense rage and anger, caused by the most trivial thing.... After subsiding, he would exhibit the greatest humility and repentance, offering the kindest and most persistent attentions...." Perhaps the saddest fact of all was that neither the prisoner's relatives nor his attorney had the slightest understanding or appreciation of his art. They had never entertained any idea of fighting the case and were concerned only with getting the accused man off as lightly as possible. Howe & Hummel, on the other hand—there might have been a difference. Producers and scenarists themselves, they would have understood perfectly Williamson's theatrical gifts and might just possibly have popped him loose.

When Williamson went to court on April twenty-sixth, the indictment read in part, "that heretofore, to wit, on the fifteenth day of February in the year of our Lord, 1880, in the city of New York, in the county of New York aforesaid, Eugene E. F. Williamson, otherwise called 'Gentleman Joe,' connived as much as in him lay to vex and annoy one Morgan Dix and with intent thereby to extort moneys from him...." The plea was guilty.

Sullivan, in his ignorance, committed the unintentional irony of calling the genius he represented a dimwit, implying mental "weakness" rather than outright madness.

"I appeal for clemency for the prisoner," he said, "as one who, in the mysterious providence of heaven, did not inherit the ordinary amount of mental strength. Just before his birth a succession of domestic calamities befell his parents. They so deeply affected his

THE RECTOR AND THE ROGUE

mother that she was under the treatment of a distinguished alienist, the late Dr. Smith of Baltimore, for several years after the prisoner was born. His conduct throughout his life has evinced the effects of the dark circumstances of his birth." A one-year sentence, Sullivan urged, would amply serve the ends of justice.

By now Williamson had been in the Tombs for a month—a terrible ordeal for the epicurean ornament of marble hotel lobbies, parlor cars, transatlantic steamers and Episcopalian pews. His chocolate-colored beard was well trimmed but his suit was no longer pressed nor were his boots polished. Most forlorn of all was the downcast expression in the once magnetic eyes. Perhaps the cruelest of the blows to strike him was public neglect, the inevitable fate of the great. No one but his lawyer came forward to speak for him. The millions in his newspaper audience, once so enthusiastic, had dropped him simply because the play was finished and the house shuttered. Even his hard-core admirers, those who understood him so well, were subject to human fickleness and had fallen away after weeks had passed. He seemed not to have a friend in the world. His relations did what they could for him, but from a distance, remaining in Pittsburgh. The prisoner at the bar was a picture of misery. "A feeling of shame seemed to have taken possession of him," the *Herald* said, "as he kept his eyes on the floor, never looking to right or left."

Judge Henry Alger Gildersleeve was a jurist long assigned to the criminal court, accustomed to dealing with gritty felons and known neither for softness of disposition nor soaring imagination. He, no more than Sullivan or anyone else, understood the caliber of the prisoner. Did the fact that Gildersleeve was a Columbia man incline him to more sympathy for Dr. Dix? Did the fact that he had been a Union major who marched with Sherman to the sea harden him a trifle toward the Confederate agent? It made no difference. The ultimate harm had already been done the prisoner. In any case, the law was the law and a two-time loser could not be treated as a first offender.

From the great height of the bench Gildersleeve looked sternly over his spectacles at the little man below. "I would be more inclined to leniency," he said, "if the defendant had learned the lesson his previous imprisonment in England should have taught him." The best Gildersleeve would do was to whittle eighteen months off the maximum term and sentence him to three and a half years at hard labor.

Williamson winced as if struck. The difference between a year's imprisonment and three and a half years would prove to be academic, since either would be a life sentence—more accurately, a death sentence. He did not know this.

"I hardly expected to get so long a term," he told reporters. "Of course I know I deserve punishment, but I don't think three years' confinement will tend to improve my morals. If they put me at hard labor I'll never live through it.... I am naturally weak, and notwithstanding that I have been guilty of a good many practical jokes, still I am not of a jovial nature and am often melancholy." Yet he tried to be jovial. "Well, perhaps I had three and a half years' worth of fun out of it," he said. But his smile was feeble, his jauntiness gone. The quip was the last he uttered. Next day, as he was handcuffed and taken by train with several other prisoners up the Hudson to Sing Sing Prison, he actually burst into tears. Unerringly he sensed that he could live only as an illicit fiction—as the Confederate colonel, the Fairfax, the English lord, the gifted poet, as Gentleman Joe and High Churchman. To destroy the myth was to destroy the man.

So the newspapers, for six weeks aquiver with a kind of drama that was unique, returned to their hackneyed routine—the runaway on Broadway, the flood in Jersey, the presentation to the city of New York by the Khedive of an obelisk called Cleopatra's Needle, the election of James Garfield. At Sing Sing, where Williamson was usually called "Your Lordship" or "The Duke" by jocular guards, he quickly became the most remarkable of the 1,567 inmates. "He was never obstinate," the *Sun* later reported, "but he gave much trouble by his peculiar methods of trying to shirk work."

The cell block, built in 1825, had five tiers of cells 7' × 3'3" × 6'6", all verminous. They were designed to provide punitive inconvenience to one inmate, but the prison was so crowded that two convicts were forced into these mere holes in a stone wall. The food, as an official commission later reported, was "unfit for human consumption." The work in the shoe factory was not utterly exhausting for a strong man but it was not to Williamson's liking, either. No one there, of course, knew the distinction of the man in their midst. Williamson himself had apparently long since passed the point where pride in his achievements in the outside world could sustain him. He soon developed a stomach ailment—the ulcers visited on sensitive souls in a hostile environment. He won the sympathy of the prison chaplain, the Reverend Dr. A. J. Edgerton, who succeeded in having him removed from hard labor and given what was regarded by the convicts as a "tea party"—duty in the prison library "assisting the chaplain in writing and pressing letters." Thus his proficiency in letter-writing was recognized to the end even if this was equivalent to making a clerk of Molière. As his malady became acute, he was removed to the prison hospital. (The staff consisted of one doctor who was likely to bleed patients for all ills.) An unidentified fellow convict assigned to the hospital related, "He said it was hard to die in such a place.... The disgrace of his punishment seemed to weigh upon him." He died December twenty-second after less than eight months' imprisonment. Chaplain Edgerton, who had been impressed by his intelligence and kindly qualities, wired the family in Pittsburgh, where Williamson ultimately was buried after a small (but very High) service at St. Andrew's.

He is the last passionate follower of Theodore Hook to be recorded, at least in the English-speaking countries. True, around the time of Williamson's trial there were a half-dozen feeble, jejune attempts to carry on the tradition in the United States, but a description of two of them suffices to show the paltriness of such performances when virtuosity is lacking. In Brooklyn, someone inserted an unauthorized HELP WANTED advertisement in a newspaper which sent twenty-seven boys seeking work to call vainly at the real-estate office of D. & M. Chauncy. And in Lancaster, Pennsylvania, a clothing merchant named George Spurrier, who was a candidate for office in the Odd Fellows, was sent a few unordered hams, pot roasts and jugs of whiskey. But the forty guests who were invited to partake (and to support Spurrier) never arrived because the postmaster became suspicious at so many postcards. He showed them to Spurrier, who made public the hoax.

These trivialities deservedly made only one-paragraph fillers for the back pages. When Hook died, a quartet of his cronies who had participated whole-heartedly in a wake held for him proposed that he be memorialized in Westminster Abbey. But of course nothing was done about it and he has since become as forgotten as Theophilus Cibber. When Williamson died, not even that drunken honor was done him. *Sic transit gloria mundi.* He did not even leave a small coterie of disciples to ponder an interesting question: since he left this world at forty, in the full flower of his talents, was it not possible that had he lived on he might have exceeded the artistry of his Dix-Buckley effort not once but several times?

As for Dr. Dix, he never seemed remotely aware that in failing to intercede for Williamson he may have had a hand in depriving posterity and the newspapers of such fascinations. He finished the memoir of his father in 1883 and soon after that gave up his losing battle against the founding of Barnard College so dangerously close to Columbia. He continued in good works and was going strong in 1905 when the sophomore class at Princeton University invented the student Joe Gish. Although Gish was non-existent, his themes and examination papers were always well done, his grades above average, and he became quite popular, being invited to party after party. His non-existence might not have been discovered for the rest of the school year had not three of his inventors carelessly signed him in at chapel the same day. Did the rector, reading of this, recall the stirring events of 1880? One doubts it, and of course it never would have occurred to him that Williamson would have applauded the hoax and would have improved on it, seeing to it that Joe Gish starred at football, led the prom, graduated with honors and secured an important position in New York. Dr. Dix died in 1908, carrying his record forty-six-year rectorship well into the twentieth century but remaining to the end an eighteenth-century man.

AUTHOR'S NOTE

This book represents a sincere effort to right a historical wrong—to restore belatedly to a great and neglected American at least a fragment of the recognition he deserves. I refer to E. Fairfax Williamson of Pittsburgh, New York, London and many other places, some of which he preferred not to mention. Nowadays the name means nothing. To be truthful, it has been virtually in oblivion for eighty-eight years. That this king of practical jokers should be so utterly lost to memory does not mean that the nation is humorless, for we have given full honor to Williamson's contemporaries in the entirely unrelated non-practical-joke field such as Bill Nye, Petroleum Nasby and Mr. Dooley.

Williamson's eclipse came about more by accident than design. He vanished like a stone dropped into the deep. In our one definitive volume on jokesters, *Hoaxes*, by Curtis D. MacDougall (New York, 1940), he is not so much as mentioned—not a word—although the Englishman Theodore Hook gets two paragraphs. To exclude Williamson from the annals of hoaxes is equivalent to writing

American history and leaving out Washington. Mr. MacDougall of course did not exclude Williamson intentionally but had simply never heard of him. No historian had ever heard of him. It is my modest hope that this cannot happen again.

This work also examines the astonishing collision (particularly at two points in history) of a moral issue and an artistic concept. It raises the question of how far the originator of an ingenious hoax is justified in imposing on a relatively few honest and long-suffering victims in order to entertain millions of people with a rich and satisfying performance that would be impossible without such imposition. Or, to reverse the proposition, should these few victims really complain when it can be shown that without their unwilling and disgruntled participation, the multitude and indeed the world would be deprived of a masterpiece? The very tone of the question betrays an unscientific bias for which I make no apology.

The picture given here of the Reverend Dr. Morgan Dix, Williamson's leading victim, is drawn from the ample records of an outstanding man who had little if anything to hide. Alas, the portrait of Williamson is less complete because he had a great deal to hide. Unlike most men who are eager to give details of their careers for publication, he kept mum because he was in trouble with the law. He wisely sought to avoid the deeper trouble that would surely follow more revelations of his past. Despite all that, it is hoped that enough emerges here to indicate the stature of the man, for never before has he been presented to the public between the covers of a book in anything but the most fragmentary way.

I first encountered the story of the persecution of Dr. Dix fully twenty years ago in *True*, then an almost unknown magazine. I thought it very funny, but it was represented as a true story and (I apologize for this weakness in faith) I wasn't having any of that because it was much too fantastic to be true. Some years later I encountered it again in abbreviated but pungent form in George

Washington Walling's *Recollections of a New York Police Chief* (New York, 1887). It *was* true! I was like the rustic suddenly convinced of the reality of the giraffe. From then on, the progress of events was swift. I researched the occurrence. Not only was it true but there was a vast fund of material untouched in the two brief published accounts—material which I seemed to be the only living person to explore. Rather than having been exaggerated, the affair had in fact been shamefully underplayed, with many of its most significant features untouched or undeveloped. For example, not even passing mention was given the Theodore Hook phenomenon, which clearly was of first importance in its effect on Williamson, nor indeed had any scrap of attention been paid to Williamson's background, character and attainments. Not a word had been published in this century about the saloonkeeper, Daniel Buckley, who easily takes his place as one of the great dupes of history.

To illustrate the full enormity of this historical negligence, there had been utter silence about two related factors which mystery writers often manufacture but which real life here had offered in overflowing fullness. One of these was the selection of Dr. Dix as the chief victim of an elaborate conspiracy—an interesting and implausible target because of his great name and reputation, innate goodness and presumed freedom from enemies. The other was the gradual discovery that if he had no personal enemies, he had literally thousands of potential enemies in many different categories because of strong moral positions he had taken and because of widespread hostility toward parish policies for which, rightly or wrongly, he could have been considered responsible. While at the outset it appeared that to plot against Morgan Dix was to plot against Red Riding Hood or Little Lord Fauntleroy, further study proved him to be regarded by many as a mixture of Scrooge, Bluebeard and the Comte de Sade. Such paradoxes are the very stuff of life for a whole school of writers who follow the lead of Agatha Christie.

Small wonder that when I discovered this great mass of long-buried information I felt an excitement akin to that of Colonel Isham at Malahide. Students of jokesmanship will understand my emotions. We can ignore those literary-historical purists who would argue that Williamson does not deserve to be mentioned in the same breath with Boswell. The Malahide Castle where I made the find was actually two places—the Yale Library newspaper room, supervised by the efficient and kindly George Nally, and the New York Public Library newspaper annex in the far reaches of West Forty-third Street. The sources perhaps lacked the romance and extreme age of the signed letters and manuscripts of the great English journal-keeper. Still, they had been preserved for over eighty years—read by millions in 1880, then put away, neglected and finally forgotten. They were, in short, the issues of New York's six most important newspapers of the era—the *Herald, Sun, Times, Tribune, World* and *Evening Post*—beginning March thirteenth and ending December twenty-sixth, 1880. All were in microfilm except for the *Post* at Yale, which still comes in great albums of blanket-sheet size. They had covered the case more thoroughly, I would guess, than anything since the Beecher scandal (which of course was of much longer duration), probably totaling at least 75,000 words on it. Even the *Post*, which was edited for stuffy intellectuals, gave it serious attention. The other five outdid themselves in chasing down witnesses and discovering new sidelights. The *Tribune* was particularly enterprising in covering the Buckley interludes, the *Herald* and the *Times* were best at dredging up background details of Williamson's career, while it was the *Sun* that took a special interest in his experiences at Sing Sing Prison and his untimely death there. *Harper's Weekly*, that pompous "journal of civilization," ignored the case entirely although it gave useless biographies of county clerks and ward politicians.

I wrote an account of the affair of perhaps 15,000 words, which I sold to the *New Yorker*. That foolish magazine sat on it for six years and never got around to printing it. While I would hesitate to say that there was a conspiracy against bringing this glowing old jewel into view, no progress was being made and meanwhile the public was being deprived of a rarity. I made a fresh appraisal of the text. The case now struck me as so unusual, so crammed with fantastic overtones, that it should be written to its full absurd length—hence this book.

I bolstered my research as far as possible. To the newspapers mentioned above was added what seems to be the only Pittsburgh paper now preserved which covers the case, the *Commercial Gazette*. The *Gazette* gives more extensive information about Williamson's activities in Pittsburgh, his family, and even a little more about his earlier career when he flitted about the world on delightfully preposterous errands. It was a valuable help, even though the *Gazette*'s files end with April 30, 1880, and thus miss his trial and imprisonment. I also enlarged my background reading to better understand the circumstances of the case and the other characters involved in it. It must be remembered that the only true source material on Williamson himself (unless I have unaccountably missed something) is the newspapers.

Most of the papers refer to him as Gentleman Jo, whereas I have used the modern spelling. In fact, exposure to Williamson's delinquencies led me to take a few other liberties which I would never dare take in dealing with more honest and prominent, if less gifted, men. For example, in a few instances I have changed speeches which appeared in the third person in the newspapers into the first person, or have joined together two quotations that were originally separated. At times which are perfectly evident I have allowed speculation to roam pretty far afield in a manner of which I am sure Eugene Fairfax Williamson would have approved, though Dr. Dix might not. Throughout the project I have been guided by the conviction that Dr. Dix has been well treated by history whereas Williamson has been not almost but *entirely and completely ignored*, and that it was my duty to redress the balance so far as I was able. Not even a photograph of him seems to exist.

Although Morgan Dix is mentioned in hundreds of publications, the most sizable published sketch of his life and career is in Volume V of *A History of the Parish of Trinity Church in the City of New York* (New York, 1950), edited by Leicester C. Lewis. Even here Williamson is slighted. He gets only a few paragraphs on pp. 138–39 and of course the attitude is biased simply because he was a criminal. The earlier volumes of this same work give Trinity's history from the very beginning, including the parish's accumulation of valuable land and its difficulties in defending it. Dix is often mentioned admiringly in the four-volume *The Diary of George Templeton Strong*, edited by Milton Halsey Thomas and Allan Nevins (New York, 1952). What a pity that Strong died before the Williamson-Dix encounter occurred! Had he still been living the case would surely have fascinated him as a lawyer and also as a highly intelligent and articulate observer. His friendship with the Dixes as well as his ingrained opposition to crime would have prejudiced him and yet one feels that he would have appreciated Williamson's talents and would have given us insights the papers missed. Morgan Dix's compilation, *The Memoirs of John Adams Dix* (two volumes, New York, 1883), tells us a great deal about that remarkable man and his family, and also about his son's great pride in him. Dr. Dix's *The Calling of a Christian Woman* (New York, 1883) illustrates beautifully his settled judgment that women, those admirable but delicate and limited creatures, should never stray far from the kitchen and nursery. Annie Nathan Meyer's *Barnard Beginnings* (Boston, 1935) tells of Dr. Dix's powerful opposition to the founding of that college but stresses the attractive courtesy with which he could clothe his anti-feminism. When he died in 1908, all the newspapers ran long obituaries containing information about him and the city's high respect for him, which never achieved communal love because of his frigid exterior. The Right Rev. William Croswell Doane, Bishop of Albany, an old friend of the rector's, preached a eulogistic sermon about him at Trinity Church on All Saints' Day, 1908, in which he offered a brief analysis of Dix's intense gravity, which made those who did not know him believe him cold. *Town Topics*, that sometimes nasty and often blackmailing publication edited by the incredible "Colonel" William D'Alton Mann, ran an interesting obituary in its May 7, 1908, issue, describing him as a great administrator but blaming him in part for the "mean, cruel parsimony of Trinity as a land-lord" and saying that he had everything the world could give him "except popularity."

The Anneke Jans Bogardus Farm (New York, 1896) was written by Stephen P. Nash, a lawyer, Trinity vestryman and friend of Morgan Dix, for the express purpose of showing Trinity's unassailable legal claim to its property and the absurdity of the many "Bogardus descendant" claims. The book was intended to put an end to such claims, but it did not, for they continued into the twentieth century. *The Golden Earth* (New York, 1935), Arthur Pound's history of Manhattan's landed wealth, devotes a chapter to the same subject, much more readable and understandable than Nash's ifs and whereases.

Emanie Sachs' *"The Terrible Siren": Victoria Woodhull* (New York, 1928) has recently been joined by two other books about the same lady, *Mrs. Satan* by Johanna Johnston and M. M. Marberry's *Vicky*, both published in New York in 1967. And Robert Shaplen's *Free Love and Heavenly Sinners* (New York, 1959) describes the manifold romantic errors of Henry Ward Beecher that left such an impress on his contemporaries, including Dr. Dix.

Two vivid books by Richard O'Connor, *Hell's Kitchen* (Philadelphia, 1958) and *The Scandalous Mr. Bennett* (New York, 1962) supply information about the Tenderloin and about James Gordon Bennett.

Junius Henri Browne's *The Great Metropolis* (New York, 1881), Herbert Asbury's *The Gangs of New York* (New York, 1930), Edward Van Every's *Sins of New York* (New York, 1930) and Dixon Wecter's *The Saga of American Society* (New York, 1937) describe various aspects of the era touched on here; and Richard Rovere's *Howe and Hummel* (New York, 1947) leaves no doubt about the illicit skills of the attorneys who might have saved Williamson had they not been given the bounce.

Handbook of American Prisons, prepared by the National Society of Penal Information (New York, 1925) gives an idea of the unpleasantness of Sing Sing Prison, where the little man spent the last sad eight months of his life. Lore about Captain Thomas F. Byrnes of the New York Police must be found piecemeal in such books as M. R. Werner's *Tammany Hall* (New York, 1928) and Bayard Veiller's *The Fun I've Had* (New York, 1941), plus a few of the sin-and-gang books mentioned in the paragraph above. Another great pity: in 1886, only six years after the Williamson-Dix case, Inspector Byrnes' (he had been promoted) massive book, *Professional Criminals of America*, was published. Does it say anything about the most fascinating malefactor Byrnes ever encountered, namely, Williamson? Not a word. Sometimes one despairs of such lack of imagination, even though Byrnes perhaps had a logical reason for excluding Gentleman Joe in the fact that he did not quite qualify as a professional criminal.

That Williamson knew the Fairfax family tree to perfection even though he had no right to climb it is shown in Thomas K. Cartmell's *The Two Fairfax Families in Virginia* (New York, 1913) and *The Fairfax Proprietary* by Joseph Look Dickinson (Front Royal, Virginia, 1959). To the two books about Theodore Hook named in the text may be added *The Choice Humorous Works of Theodore Hook* (anonymous, London, n.d.), which also contains a sketch of his life.

My sincere thanks for the warm cooperation of Sarah Mitchell and Elizabeth Downs, librarian and assistant librarian of our own unequaled small-town library in Newtown, Connecticut. And to S. Rex Green of St. Paul, Minnesota, my deep gratitude for countless kindnesses.

W. A. S.

AFTERWORD

The Rector and the Rogue first came into my hands some ten years ago, and quite from out of the blue—rather like a letter from Gentleman Joe himself. I was working in the Welsh "book town" of Hay-on-Wye, and found it atop a pile of miscellany that had been disgorged from a shipping container. Random auction lots descend upon peculiar Welsh villages with some frequency; this one contained the final remains of some shuttered library in Coral Gables, Florida. I started reading and became so engrossed that I neglected the rest of my shift. A whole other mystery engulfed me as I read further into the book: How had I never heard of Gentleman Joe or his "peculiar campaign of botheration"? And how had I never heard of *The Rector and the Rogue*?

It was not for a lack of trying by the author. Although largely out of print today, William Andrew Swanberg (1907–1992) had risen to the top of his field when this book came out in 1968. After years as a book editor, he'd authored a series of tart historical narratives that won him acclaim, and then a certain notoriety as the first author to ever have a Pulitzer Prize vetoed. The prize's trustees struck down the Pulitzer jury's unanimous decision to award Swanberg for his biography *Citizen Hearst* on the grounds that Hearst—who had been Joseph Pulitzer's mortal enemy—did not embody "patriotic and unselfish services to the people." Swanberg would find himself in excellent company: the following year the trustees vetoed the jury's prize to Edward Albee for *Who's Afraid of Virginia Woolf?*; not much later, they also struck down an award to Duke Ellington. But eventually Swanberg would get a Pulitzer—in 1972, this time for a biography of Henry Luce—as well as a Guggenheim Fellowship and a National Book Award.

While Swanberg's other biographies have long since been superceded by later efforts, *The Rector and the Rogue* remains unique. It is the first and still the only account of this affair. But beyond being an entertaining story, something about Gentleman Joe has sent me back to this book every year or two since I first found it. Here was someone taking the daily penny post and mass-circulation classified ads, and using them to attack the head of an institution. Here was a man, operating under a false name and in a rented room, subverting public communication technologies to create chaos—and doing this purely for the hell of it.

———————

Swanberg died in 1992, still hard at work on his next book. He just missed the dawning of the Internet era—the first hypertext web browser, Lynx, had been created only a few months before. We now live in a golden age of information for historians—one Swanberg would have reveled in—and yet combing through modern databases reveals just how resourceful of a researcher he was. I find remarkably few stones left unturned in his account of Gentleman Joe's campaign. I can, however, shed a bit more light on what happened before and after that fateful collision of rector and rogue.

EXTRAORDINARY PERSECUTIONS, announced an issue of *Reynold's Newspaper* for August 3rd, 1873. The persecution, of course, is that of Mr. Adolph Rosenbaum of 1 Bloomsbury Square, a diamond merchant and former landlord of Eugene Fairfax Williamson. Williamson's letters, ominously signed REVENGE and VENGEANCE, demanded a payment of fifty guineas, a sum to rise to seventy if not met within a week. But as he would also later claim in the Reverend Dix case, Williamson's defense was that he never seriously intended to collect any money; already having £161 on his person when arrested, "he was in possession of ample means, and therefore could have no object in seeking to extort money," the *Pall Mall Gazette* reported. Williamson narrowly escaped the severe charge of a financial crime, and was imprisoned instead for harassment; he promised the judge that "he was now perfectly sensible of the folly of his conduct."

"I was treated very kindly," he recalled to a *New York Tribune* reporter, when asked in April 1880 about his London imprisonment. "I was in the 'N.L.'—no labor—class. You know they have two classes—those who work and those who don't."

He would not find the State of New York quite so forgiving.

"A disease of the stomach" was how a brief notice in the *Tribune* would characterize Gentleman Joe's death in Sing Sing just eight months later. But hidden deep within the historical record is a more disturbing story of how he met his end. When Swanberg notes that prison guards addressed Williamson as "His Lordship" and "The Duke," there may have been a hint of malevolence in their voices. For just two years later, a former guard revealed that Gentleman Joe's death did not sound much like a stomach disease at all—and a lot more like homicide.

"That man," testified Elihu Campbell before a State Assembly committee, "was driven into consumption and finally death."

The hearings had come about from the shocking accusations made by Campbell in a *Tribune* exposé of Sing Sing—a sensational article that had as one of its prime examples the fate of one Eugene Fairfax Williamson.

"The first time I saw him he didn't look like a mechanic," Campbell recalled. "Of course he wasn't robust; he looked like a fellow that had never done any hard work."

Williamson was immediately placed in the worst job in the prison: the emery room, where prisoners operated grinding and polishing wheels. It was a virtual death sentence: the room, billowing clouds of dust, had no ventilation. "Those men standing there, you couldn't see them," the jailer testified. "You couldn't tell a black man from a white man." Williamson was given the very hardest pieces to grind and polish: small knobs no larger than his thumb. It did not go well—"he ground the end of his fingers off," Campbell recalled—and to punish his incompetence, Williamson was stripped naked, hung from the ceiling by his wrists, and beaten savagely with wooden paddles.

It wasn't long, the jailer admitted, before Williamson "looked like he was all racked to pieces." Three days before Christmas, the prisoner dragged himself to the infirmary and begged to be let in. His reputation as a trickster, though, had already preceded him. "I know you," the prison's doctor snapped and turned him away. "You are playing sick to get hospital rations. You can't fool me." But Gentleman Joe had indeed fooled him—for he died in his cell that very night.

His mischief, though, may have only just begun.

———

I have a suspicion regarding our old prankster, and to explain it, let me start—rather in the manner of the old Gent himself—by making an outrageous accusation against a wealthy and respectable public figure in New York City.

Mayor Bloomberg is a squatter.

This, at least, is the upshot of claims by the descendants of Robert Edwards, an 18th century Welsh buccaneer whose progeny now thickly populate the United States, Britain, and Australia. They have spent over a century contending that the Edwards family owned a large tract of Manhattan, land which in 1778 his family supposedly leased to Trinity Church on a ninety-nine-year agreement.

A later copy of the alleged lease reads:

Manhattan Island

June 1, 1778

Know all men by these presents: That I, Robert Edwards, on this day lease to John and George Cruger 77 acres 3 rods and 32 erches, beginning in the stake set in the ground at the high water mark, near Bestavern, Fittlegil, and running East along Prince Street 1,000 feet; thence Northwesterly in a zigzag course along part of Old Jans land to Christopher Street to high water mark 547 feet; thence South along the Hudson River along the lines of high water mark 2,276 feet to the point and place of the beginning. Said land being leased for 99 years at 1,000 pounds and a pepper corn yearly rental. Said land to be held by John and George Cruger and their heirs so long as contract is fulfilled; otherwise it must revert to me and my living heirs, and at the expiration of the 99 years lease said land together with all improvements shall revert to my lawful heirs, which will be descendants of my brothers and sister which are as follows: William Edwards, Jacob Edwards, Leonard Edwards, Joshua Edwards, John Edwards, Thomas Edwards and Martha Edwards.

Witness my hand and seal this June 1, 1778.

Robert S.E. Edwards, John Cruger, George Cruger

Witness: Anthony Barclay, Nicholas Bayard

The land in question, according to the Edwards heirs, encompasses Wall Street, Greenwich Village, and—in their more excitable moments—even the land underneath City Hall. Its value is some-times cited as some $680 billion dollars.

The problem? The Edwards say that Trinity never gave the land back.

Alas, courts have not looked kindly on the put-upon pirates. Attempts in the 1890s at mounting a court case went awry; later attempts in 1931, 1954, and 1966 were dismissed as without merit. All along, con artists preyed upon the hopes of Edwards heirs; in a 1999 racketeering case, the founder of the Pennsylvania Edwards Heirs Association was found guilty of embezzling at least $650,000 from Edwards descendants, which went into purchasing a Mercedes Benz, bulletproof vests, payments to mistresses, and a trip to Disney World.

It hardly helps that no one has been able to find the original deed or lease. An internal 1989 memo in Trinity's files remarks incredulously:

> Every likelihood suggests that Edwards-Cruger lease never existed. Notice to produce the lease was given in the Robert Reed case [of 1931], but it was never complied with. The explanation offered in that case for the failure to produce the lease... have a nightmare quality. The lease is reported as having been present in the Register's Office when the searcher first appeared at the office, but the custodian of the particular safe in which the lease was kept away for the morning or afternoon but would produce it when he returned the following day. The searcher accepts the explanation and goes, returning on the following day, only to be told that the Edwards-Cruger lease has unaccountably disappeared...

Trinity Church, by contrast, does possess an original 1705 land grant from Queen Anne. But that is hardly the point: the entire case is pure humbug. Even if the Edwards heirs found their fabled lease, the doctrine of adverse possession (squatter's rights) means they long since relinquished the land to Trinity.

The result is a perfect meeting of an Unmovable Object (Trinity, and its absolute claim upon the land) and an Irresistible Force (the lure of countless billions should the heirs ever succeed). But there's never been a theory as to why the Edwards Heirs case first came about. As early as 1896 the case was such old hat that the *New York Tribune* could refer to "numerous and foolish" Edwards Heirs seeking "phantasmal millions." Edwards Heirs are noted in the *New York Times* as far back as 1883; another contemporary account notes they'd begun organizing "beginning in 1880." That they had no original copy of the lease to organize around did not deter them; there was only a much argued-over later copy of indistinct provenance. But if it's not real, who would have bothered to invent that document in the first place?

Well: who is the one man we know was forging Trinity-related documents in 1880?

I believe the Edwards Heirs are the last and greatest hoax of Gentleman Joe. He has the means and motive; he is the right man in the right place at the right time. The Edwards Heirs materialized just as Williamson was tormenting Trinity with his brilliantly unhinged campaign of hundreds of forged letters. He'd have operated with the common local knowledge that at least one previous clan (the Bogardus family) had a long-standing claim against the church; indeed, newspapers had revived their coverage of that case in May 1879, exactly when the very first Gentleman Joe forgery appeared. And newspapers were already filled with dark allegations about the church's other land dealings. So the Edwards story would arrive to a public who thought that it could conceivably be true: a vital ingredient for any successful hoax. One spurious "copy" of a newly expired lease, and a few whispered rumors, are all it would have taken to set into motion what has turned out to be a century-long legal avalanche.

It seems a quaint trick to have legions of pawnbrokers and tattooists showing up at a rector's door. And yet every decade or two for the last 130 years, hundreds of would-be plaintiffs have gathered in meeting halls and courtrooms, as benighted as any rabble of misdirected undertakers, and all to torment every successor to the Reverend Morgan Dix. Trinity has been getting dunned by wild letters for over a century now, and I truly believe they will still be getting them a century hence. The hoax is perfect—it is immortal—for as long as there is a mankind to be fooled, and Manhattan land to be fooled about, it can never die.

Somewhere among the shades, perhaps, one can still hear Gentleman Joe having a very hearty laugh.

Paul Collins
Portland, Oregon
January 2011